BRIEF THERAPEUTIC CONSULTATIONS

WILEY SERIES
in
BRIEF THERAPY AND COUNSELLING

Editor
Windy Dryden

Brief Rational Emotive Behaviour Therapy
Windy Dryden

Brief Therapeutic Consultations
An approach to systemic counselling
Eddy Street and Jim Downey

Brief Therapy with Couples
Maria Gilbert and Diane Shmukler

Further titles in preparation

BRIEF THERAPEUTIC CONSULTATIONS

An approach to systemic counselling

Eddy Street and Jim Downey

JOHN WILEY & SONS

Chichester · New York · Brisbane · Toronto · Singapore

Copyright © 1996 by John Wiley & Sons Ltd,
Baffins Lane, Chichester,
West Sussex PO19 1UD, England

National   01243 779777
International   (+44) 1243 779777
e-mail (for orders and customer service enquiries): cs-book@wiley.co.uk
Visit our Home Page on http://www.wiley.co.uk
or http://www.wiley.com

Other Wiley Editorial Offices

John Wiley & Sons, Inc., 605 Third Avenue,
New York, NY 10158-0012, USA

Jacaranda Wiley Ltd, 33 Park Road, Milton,
Queensland 4064, Australia

John Wiley & Sons (Canada) Ltd, 22 Worcester Road,
Rexdale, Ontario M9W 1L1, Canada

John Wiley & Sons (Asia) Pte Ltd, 2 Clementi Loop #02-01,
Jin Xing Distripark, Singapore 0512

Library of Congress Cataloging-in-Publication Data

Street, Eddy.
    Brief therapeutic consultations : an approach to systemic counselling / Eddy Street and Jim Downey.
        p.   cm. — (Wiley series in brief therapy and counselling)
    Includes bibliographical references and index.
    ISBN 0-471-96343-7 (pbk. : alk. paper)
    1. Brief psychotherapy.   2. Counselling.   I. Downey, Jim.
    II. Title.   III. Series.
    RC480.55.S77   1996   96–21695
                                                       CIP

British Library Cataloguing in Publication Data

A catalogue record for this book is available from the British Library

ISBN 0-471-96343-7

Typeset in 10/12pt Palatino from the author's disk by Dorwyn Ltd, Rowlands Castle, Hants
Printed and bound in Great Britain by Bookcraft (Bath) Ltd., Midsomer Norton, Somerset
This book is printed on acid-free paper responsibly manufactured from sustainable forestation, for which at least two trees are planted for each one used for paper production.

CONTENTS

ABOUT THE AUTHORS

Eddy Street is a chartered counselling and clinical psychologist. He is currently working for an NHS Trust where his clinical work covers a range of problems that can befall children. He has a special interest working with families that are dealing with handicapping conditions and the effects of trauma and abuse.

He has published widely, having written numerous chapters and articles on the themes of family counselling with particular relevance to child focused problems. He is the author of *Counselling for Family Problems* (1994, Sage, London).

He is a regular contributor to radio on matters connected with families.

Jim Downey is a chartered clinical psychologist working in South Wales. He has recently returned to work as a full time clinician in a specialist mental health NHS trust. Prior to this he was the child and family specialist tutor to the South Wales doctoral course in clinical psychology. He has published in several journals and contributed to a number of books. He has a particular interest in the development and evaluation of counselling and consultation services to various client groups.

SERIES PREFACE

In recent years, the field of counselling and psychotherapy has become preoccupied with brief forms of intervention. While some of this interest has been motivated by expediency – reducing the amount of help that is offered to clients to make the best use of diminishing resources – there has also developed the view that brief therapy may be the treatment of choice for many people seeking therapeutic help. It is with the latter view in mind that the Wiley Series in Brief Therapy and Counselling was developed.

This series of practical texts considers different forms of brief therapy and counselling as they are practised in different settings and with different client groups. While no book can substitute for vigorous training and supervision, the purpose of the books in the present series is to provide clear guides for the practice of brief therapy and counselling, which is here defined as lasting 25 sessions or less.

Windy Dryden
Series Editor

PREFACE

No one's mouth is big enough to utter the whole thing.
                                                Alan Watts (1957)

Over the past decade or so we have witnessed the emergence of a much more vigorous consumer voice. This is particularly relevant to any citizen who is the customer or client of an institutional or a professional's service. It has been suggested that the increased public access to information, achieved via all forms of the communicative media, has raised the citizen's awareness of his/her own rights and powers; in addition, the institutions and professions operate with a greater sensitivity to their more accountable position. It has also introduced the notion of relationships with clients that are based on equality and transparency.

The change in citizens' status and power is a process which now appears to be feeding off itself. Consumer lobby groups in every area of professional practice are promoting change in the traditional relationship between the public and the professions. The evidence of change is present not only in consumer action groups, but also in recent Acts of legislation which incorporate within their general principles the idea of increased citizens' rights and institutional responsibilities and accountability. The Education Acts (1988, 1993), The Children Act (1989), and the Access to Health Records Act (1990) all enshrine these principles. These legislative changes are also supported by political initiatives such as The Citizen's Charter and The Patient's Charter. There has also been seen an increasing interest in the private and public sectors in the idea that user or consumer satisfaction and indicators of service quality are now important areas of evaluation. This makes them an expected area of concern within any modern-thinking and ethically responsible organization or service . These changes are not confined to the commercial world but are also evident in the thinking and practices of therapeutic and counselling professions.

One also has to see these changes in light of the organizational change that is taking place inside the caring professions in Britain. The application of the market place to the provision of health care is another of these major changes and indeed it is the desire to set up the purchaser–provider model that has led to the metamorphis of client to consumer. Another corollary of this way of thinking is the emphasizing of the family being the sole social organization which should bear the financial and/or practical care of the ill, young, sick, elderly and needy.

All these processes have an implication for the practice of counselling, as societal forces undoubtedly shape the practice of psycho-therapeutic endeavours. This certainly has been the case for us in the development of this model. The ideas which we present in this volume have not come from a group of therapists isolated in some ivory tower wishing to push to the leading edge of theory, for it is the response of a group of health-care practitioners struggling to find their way in the maelstrom of change that surrounds them.

Our initial work on these ideas were when we were constituted as The Family and School Age Children Psychology Services Team (FASS Team) which was composed of ourselves and Anna Brazier. At that time our desire was to present a menu of services to families which they could select from a position of 'informed consent'. We also wished to do this in a way that provided a degree of uniformity from within our rather idiosyncratic and individualistic practices. By the method of clinical comparison, sharing cases and discussing outcomes and auditing our work in a general way, we slowly developed a particular way of working. We initially presented these ideas in a paper entitled 'The development of therapeutic consultations in child focused family work' (Street *et al.*, 1991). Our application of this approach found resonances in other services and contexts. Via our contact with different professional groups in training we discovered an applicability of the approach to situations familiar to employee assistant programmes, private marital work, individual counselling in public agencies and as always the provision of services to families struggling with parental difficulties. In a number of respects we found that when teaching the approach the students not only gained an appreciation of a different set of counselling skills but they also developed a more systemic understanding of the context of their professional role. This we have seen as an unintended benefit. We therefore see the development of this model as not being the production of another way of being a counsellor but an extension of counselling skills themselves – skills which can only be located in the individual practitioner's particular context. This approach is therefore a way of presenting a counselling service rather than being a service itself.

As these ideas were originally developed in a clinical fashion we have constructed the book in such a way that theories which informed their expression are presented towards the rear of the text (Chapter 7). We further explain this in the body of the book in Chapter 1 in which the notion of consultation is elaborated. The bulk of the book Chapters 2–6 contain the practical details of embarking on this approach. Our suggestion to readers is that they should dip in and out of the theoretical section in a way which suits their style of learning. Within the book we make constant use of clinical examples and there are some extended clinical examples which run across the first six chapters. All these examples are fictitious in that we have constructed them specifically to illustrate the points we make. However, in nearly all respects we have met the examples which we provide; they are familiar to us and hopefully in the problems they present they will be familiar to other practitioners. Should there be anyone who finds that elements of their personal life appear too similar to the examples then we apologize for this. It is by no means intended and merely is an indication of the similarity of the human predicament in modern western society.

We should like to acknowledge the important contribution Anna Brazier made when we were in the process of constructing these ideas; we are very appreciative of her help and involvement. Sue Palmer, Jayne Salisbury and Hannah Steer undertook various follow-up projects on our clinical work; we are grateful for this as it provided much valuable information. Special thanks to Anne Flower who for the lifetime of FASS was its excellent secretary; her role was an essential element in the smooth running of our service. Amongst her many tasks she found time to type the initial drafts of the manuscript and we would like to extend our sincere appreciation to her for all she did for us. Thanks also to Chris Cureton for her organizational skills as this project neared completion and also to Mark Rivett who helped by reading particular sections and providing us with some good ideas. We are both greatly indebted to our families, particularly our wives, who supported us, encouraged us, and generally created the caring space which allowed us to indulge our creativity and carry out the practical tasks that followed. Finally we should like to record our thanks and affection for each other. We have closely worked together for over a decade and the processes that led to the development of this approach also led to the disbanding of FASS and personal moves that have meant we are now working in different places. We are both pleased and proud that this book is a tangible testament to our professional collabaration which has been greatly enjoyable for us and hopefully beneficial to our clients.

Eddy Street   Jim Downey
Cardiff, September 1995

FOR ANNA AND ALYSON

CONSULTATION AND COUNSELLING

BY WAY OF INTRODUCTION

This book is written by two practising clinicians/counsellors whose daily work involves them in many and various client counselling relationships. Our principal 'client' is the family with dependent children and in this area of work our counselling practice is guided and organized by developmental and systemic ideas. However, even in this clinical area we are often required to establish an individual client focus, e.g. when we feel it is most appropiate or when the family requires it of us, and we have still found the developmental and systemic perspectives to be valuable in the construction of the counselling relationship. We will be returning to these ideas in greater detail later.

We work in settings which for the present appear to be suffering constant changes in their organization and managerial procedures which of course have an impact upon the clinical context. The increasing workload, primarily clinical referrals and administrative tasks, plus the increasing organizational demand for demonstrable evidence of service effectiveness and economy, made us concerned about our clinical practice and about that group of clients who 'dropped out of treatment' or 'ceased to attend counselling' before we felt a satisfactory conclusion had been reached. Our consternation about the comparatively high proportion of 'defaulters' – between 25 and 35 per cent – led us to go one step further and we undertook a small survey of clients – representing both completed counselling contacts (i.e. agreed client/professional closure) and incompleted counselling contacts (i.e. client ceased to attend without explanation and/or before the counsellor felt a point had been reached at which termination was appropriate) and those who did not attend for a first appointment. The survey, although falling short of the requirements of a formal, empirical piece of work nevertheless provided us with a range of client responses which we found interesting.

Our client group indicated that how they perceived the counsellor (and the service context), in terms of attractiveness, competence, style, etc. were relevant to ongoing attendance. However, more important in terms of implications for practice were the indications that:

- Clients had an idea of what it was they wished to achieve from the contact.
- Clients appeared to arrive in initial sessions with expectations of how we, the professional, would act in response to their account/their difficulty.

We are not the first counsellors to 'discover' that clients attend counselling sessions with expectations which appear to influence the course of counselling (Garfield, 1982). Like others before us then our survey findings led us to reflect upon the area and the issue of how to respond or deal with 'the client's pre-contact expectations of the counsellor'. From our identification of this specific area, we found ourselves embarking upon a quite fundamental reconsideration of how we conceived of and constructed the very first contact(s) of the counselling relationship. The development of our own counselling practice, which is described in this book, is the practical outcome of those reflections.

The approach described does not aim, nor claim, to revolutionize counselling practice nor does it outline some grand new theory of counselling. Its ambition is humbler in that it suggests a broader view of the client–counsellor relationship, such that the earliest contacts are constructed as being outside of the counselling context in a strict sense. The initial professional relationship offered to the client is then more properly described as constituting 'a consultation to the client'. As we explain later, we are severe in our assertion that this contact does not represent the 'early stages of counselling'. It is in conceptual and practical terms vital that it is seen as a distinct area of activity and relationship which contributes to the client's decision-making about their difficulty. Furthermore, and as we will explain more fully later, we believe it is correct to call this type of contact a consultation because the client's agenda is the only basis for professional comment. There is no presumption, on our part, of hidden, superior or altruistic agendas. Moreover, it is our view that any contact between client and another which is based upon an empathic, understanding, valuing and respectful attitude will perforce be therapeutic. Therefore the type of counsellor–client contact to be described here is called 'a therapeutic consultation' and we believe it represents *an extension of the counsellor's range of activities*. We acknowledge this is not an entirely new therapeutic idea: earlier Winnicott (1971) made use of the term to describe a particular type of paediatric contact; latterly Wynne *et al.* (1987) have discussed the notion of pre-treatment consultation. However, it is a feature of this approach that the consultation is described entirely by the aim of facilitating the client's next decision in relation to their problem-centred story with this being its overriding purpose. In essence the approach is composed of one or two consultation interviews organized relatively close together and a follow-up interview preplanned at a time a distance away from the initial meeting(s). A distinctive element in the practice is the sending of a 'consultation letter' to the client which summarizes the main points from the interviews. Once we began to adopt this practice we were surprised by the considerable reduction in the numbers of defaulters and the general increase in reported satisfaction by our clients post-contact. It is this model of practice that we present in this book.

Organization of This Book

In writing this book we have attempted to separate what might be called the 'heavy' theoretical background from the practical aspects of the approach. We believe there are many ways of justifying this method of working and we do not wish to suggest that how we arrived at this point is the only way. Different readers will understand what we have to say in different ways which in part will be dependent upon their existing models and methods of working. Our hope is that by separating the theoretical from the practical the reader will be helped to avoid the mistake of perceiving them as inevitably and inextricably entwined. In the process of this model's development we found theory often followed clinical insight and in this sense the approach is grounded in our experience as clinicians/counsellors and not as empirical scientists. Our guiding paradigm and method has therefore been post-modern (see The Social Constructionist View of the Counsellor–Client Relationship, p. 116) Nevertheless it is the case that some of the ideas expressed and, we believe, conveyed by the consultative approach, are theoretically traceable (e.g. systemic and developmental theory), and they are therefore included as a theoretical 'appendix' to the book in Chapter 7. The reader is invited to refer to the theoretical section whenever and wherever they feel it may be helpful to their own understanding of the idea of the therapeutic consultation. Apart from the temporally sequenced flow of the clinical examples the sections of this book can be read in any order.

We begin with an outline of one of the principal thrusts to recent developments in counselling, namely the movement toward 'brief' approaches, and then we introduce the reader to the notion of 'consultation'.

BRIEFLY FORWARD

At the present time with so many variations on the therapeutic/ counselling theme it is easy to confuse 'forms' of counselling activity which represent important advances in the general field with less significant or unsupported diversions. Since the late 1970s various therapeutic schools have questioned the client-transforming objective of traditional therapeutic relationships and the accompanying necessity for lengthy counselling contacts. One general response has been the development of various versions of brief therapy or counselling; from the psychoanalytic brief therapy of Balint *et al.* (1972) to the brief solution-focused family therapy of de Shazer *et al.* (1986) (see Brief Family Therapy, p. 142). The primary impetus for the development of briefer forms of counselling may not have been entirely altruistic or client led as the increasing demand on counselling services located in the public sector and the cost-conscious private sector has certainly provided some of the stimulation. Overall, however, the development of the brief approach does appear to have some basis in the client's experience of and response to longer forms of counselling which frequently appeared to pursue objectives principally set by the counsellor. The brief therapy movement now appears to be transtheoretical in that its basic tenets and principles of practice can be encompassed by most schools of therapy. Its origins are probably to be discovered in the influential findings of adult psychotherapists such as Bloom (1992) and Mann (1984) (see Therapeutic Ideas Relevant to Therapeutic Consultations, p. 142). They based the development of their practice on an extensive review of the therapy outcome literature available in the 1960s and 1970s which found that planned, short-term individual adult therapy produced outcomes equal or superior to the outcomes of longer-term therapy. This linked to another area of research interest that revealed that short-term therapy appears to fit with the expectations people entering therapy have about the length of therapy. Empirical studies have also consistently found that client satisfaction is not linked to length of therapy. Littlepage (1976) and Silverman and Beech (1979) both found, in follow-up surveys of people who had unilaterally terminated therapy after a few sessions, that satisfaction with the therapy experience was consistently high. Indeed there are findings to suggest that longer-term therapy appears to be associated with 'diminishing returns' in terms of client change (Howard *et al.*, 1986) with most change occurring in the earliest contacts.

Research into the value of short- versus long-term therapy has also found an echo in more recent work which appropriately focuses on the client's experience of counselling (Llewelyn, 1988) and on the client's view of their mental health concerns (Foulks *et al.*, 1986; Pistrang and Barker, 1992). The vital importance of attending to the client's expectations and perceptions is indicated by an increasing number of studies which strongly underline the likelihood of 'better' outcomes (as defined by the client) being achieved in counselling relationships that are congruent with the client's own beliefs and expectations (Atkinson *et al.*, 1991; Brewin and Bradley, 1989). In total accord with these findings are studies (Patterson and Forgatch, 1985; Miller, 1989) which suggest that counsellor actions perceived by the client as directive, coercive, or confrontational are much more likely to evoke resistance in the client and can be associated with a poor counselling outcome. These factors have a relevance across approaches as the way in which the counsellor and client interact and experience the relationship appears to be more important to outcome than the specific approach or school of thought from which the counsellor operates (Stiles, *et al.*, 1986). The factors which best account for positive change in clients are clearly related more to characteristics of the relationship between client and counsellor than to any other specific treatment procedures or activities.

The plain suggestion coming from various reviews (Ursano and Hales, 1986; Budman, 1981) and more recently supported by findings in British studies, (Llewelyn, 1988; Stiles *et al.*, 1990) is that most clients want the counsellor to be understanding, to give practical advice about resolving their difficulty and to achieve positive change within a few sessions. This contrasts with the general view once held by most therapists that short-term contacts are unlikely to achieve lasting change, that there is a need for the client to achieve insight and understanding into their problems and that the termination of therapy should be a therapist or joint decision. The general findings in fact suggest that a very brief contact between client and counsellor, wherein the client is listened to and asked pertinent personal questions, seems to assist in promoting positive change. The positive outcome, furthermore, does not appear closely related to the specific model of the counsellor, their experience or level of skill.

A plausible and to us a compelling conclusion to be drawn is that the client, in coming to the appointment, has already embarked upon a process of active change (see Stages of Change Model, p. 139). It seems likely then that the counsellor in his/her actions can either facilitate that change process by linking with powerful client change tendencies or can obstruct client momentum principally by seeking to develop counsellor inspired goals for the client which may not be understood or accepted by them.

This summary of the research findings would appear particularly appropriate when applied to the ambivalence usually found in clients when they first encounter a counsellor. The client who enters the counselling relationship with a degree of ambivalence in respect of the problem and its solution is probably the typical client and the one most easily lost by early, ill-advised and counsellor-controlled action. Ambivalence is neither a sign of abnormality nor a serious threat to the client making sensible decisions. A more serious threat it seems to us is embodied in the over-eager and too knowledgeable expert who may take instant recourse to offering advice, information and/or ongoing counselling without first establishing the client's own position (Miller, 1985; Patterson and Frogatch, 1985).

In our view therefore a successful client–counsellor contact is heavily dependent on the counsellor achieving a good understanding of the client's expectations and perceptions of the professional service to be offered as well as an understanding of the client's own perception of their particular situation. Counsellor activity which is congruent with both the client's model of 'professional action' and their view of the difficulty which brings them is more likely to be experienced as appropriate and satisfying by the client and for many clients this contact will be brief.

We consider that these aims are adequately achieved within the notion of *therapeutic consultations*. In particular, there is an implicit belief that has to be maintained above all else and that is that the client has an idea of what it is they want from the contact with the counsellor/consultant. They are in charge of defining the problem, the goal and to an extent the role to be played by the professional.

WHY CONSULTATION?

We have categorized our approach as a consultation between a client and a professional. We do not construe it as counselling, a prelude to counselling or an early phase of counselling. We propose that it is a distinct and separate activity from a range of possible client/professional relationships. As such it is defined and embodied in the professional's understanding of the relationship he or she is being invited to enter with the client. In itself, it may be complete and sufficient; alternatively it may lead onto a differently constructed relationship between client and professional of which counselling is but one possibility. There is in this social constructionist perspective a vital difference between the relationship offered in consultation and that offered in traditional counselling. (see The Social Constructionist view of the Counsellor–Client Relationship, p. 116). To amplify these points and as a preface to our clinical approach we shall briefly discuss some of the cardinal features of the counselling relationship and contrast them with the central elements of the consultation relationship.

'Problems' in the Counselling Context

The client/counsellor relationship is founded upon an acceptance and understanding by the participants of their designated roles. In the counselling relationship the client is designated as in 'need' and the counsellor is designated the 'expert' who will address and satisfy client need. In doing so, client and counsellor enter a relationship which is clearly based upon a complementary difference in power. The counsellor is expected to have knowledge and skills which allows him/her to maximize what is 'best' for the client in respect of their particular difficulty. The client, in the counselling relationship, is therefore a *help-seeker* and the counsellor an expert help-giver. The counselling process and relationship structure might therefore be formally described as 'medical–collaborative'. (see Models of Helping, p. 137). Firstly it seeks to work *with* the client rather than working *on* the client (collaborative). Secondly it rests upon a belief that the counsellor knows best and will, if necessary, persuade the client to accept a more 'helpful' or 'hopeful' view of their personal dilemma and of the best course(s) of action to take in the circumstances (medical).

The respected and widely used three-stage model of counselling developed by Egan (1990), illustrates the point for in the initial construction of the relationship, as indicated by Egan, the counsellor pursues an *implicit* goal of *persuading* the client to accept the counsellor's view of the problem and solution. The counsellor has a task of persuasion, of converting the client to a 'better' way of seeing things. This is justified by reference to the client's assumed consent to 'treatment', the altruistic objectives and intent of the counselling and the counsellor's expertise and expert knowledge.

This representative model of counselling highlights two separate but related major criticisms of counselling practice. The first concerns the notion of informed consent. Hoffman (1990) in an important discursive paper spoke of 'therapy by stealth' by which she meant those counselling relationships which develop around the client without the client really being aware and certainly not formally notified by the counsellor, that counselling (of them) has begun. Hoffman raises an uncomfortable but important professional and ethical question which is posed when 'unannounced' counselling occurs. It is unwarranted and unprofessional for counsellors to act as if the client has already appraised and chosen counselling as their next step in dealing with their difficulty. The nature of consent can therefore be problematic. Even when clients attend asking for counselling it is the ethical duty of the counsellor (as expert in the professional system) to explore the process which has led to the making of the decision, to make the client aware of the other professional service options open to them, in order that the client's choice is as informed as possible.

The second major issue concerns the origin of the proposed direction of change. Clearly counselling, whilst being attentive, empathic and sensitive to client concerns, is also constructed to achieve an outcome of *client change*. The direction and manner of change will to a large extent depend upon the counsellor's personal preferences and theoretically informed judgement. Indeed, it has been demonstrated that a process of client persuasion and eventual conversion to the counsellor's way of seeing their problem is at the heart of successful counselling (Strong, 1968). The aim of facilitating someone's self-improvement is laudable and fundamentally altruistic but it can also be a form of extreme paternalism or at worst a form of oppression based on the power and authority of the counsellor. As the whole aim of counselling is towards helping clients achieve personal self-enhancing change, this core objective is therefore shown to be challengeable and not beyond serious enquiry

It is not our argument that counselling should cease because of these criticisms, on the contrary it is an activity that professionally needs to continue and we shall continue to engage in it. Our perspective is that the assumptions surrounding and supporting the practice of counselling can lead and have led to the misuse of expert power. Unless we practise with complete awareness of the social context in which counselling is constructed we practise at our own and our clients' peril. We believe to deny or neglect this would detract from our ideals of professional conduct and result in potentially unethical practice.

Consultation: an Alternative Construction

Consultation and the consultant's role offers a position and relationship to the counsellor which allows the client to make informed decisions about how they wish to proceed. It begins by regarding the client as an active enquirer i.e. an 'information seeker' rather than as a 'help-seeker'. In establishing a (therapeutic) space for a consultation relationship we believe the consultant is more likely to satisfy the requirements of a profession whose quintessential concern is with promoting and assisting clients in the development and maintenance of self-agency through personal choice and decision-taking. Clearly a consultation begins with the very initial contact between counsellor and client, even arguably at the point of referral, and is particularly concerned with how the consultant receives the client and his/her account of the difficulty, and how the consultant presents what he/she (or others) can offer.

We perceive the process of consultation as being potentially therapeutic but that does not constitute it as being a process that can be termed 'therapy' or 'counselling'. It uses skills derived from counselling and therapy models (see Therapeutic ideas relevant to Therapeutic Consultations, p. 142) and beneficial outcomes may accrue at its completion. Indeed many professions have adopted the term 'Consultation' to describe various areas of professional activity. The concept of consultation which is intended here is probably most closely represented in the organizational consultation model rather than that of the medical consultation. From the world of organizational research, Gallessich (1985) has discussed the characteristic features of the consultation process;

1. Consultation is a process initiated and *owned* by the client.
2. It is a starting point for the client and consultant to explore and establish the professional services which could be rendered.
3. The consultant's duty is to establish an explicit framework to the relationship which allows the consultee to 'state their case', whilst by its overt structure, making clear how and what the consultant needs to know and intends to do as part of the consultation.
4. The consultation is primarily concerned with the establishment of a collaborative relationship. Its content is predominantly that of information exchange, clarification and the achievement of a shared understanding. The relationship is symmetrical rather than complementary, i.e. client and consultant are equal but different.

Keeping in mind that this list refers to organisational consultation, it will be seen that it incorporates many features which are familiar to the counselling context. However, the vital difference lies in the fact that the consultant does not assume, either overtly or covertly, that a personal 'change' formula is a professional goal or responsibility. What follows the whole process and development of the consultation is something for the client to decide.

In addition to outlining the central features of the consultation, Gallessich (1985) also suggested that there are three principal ideological systems (sets of belief) underpinning consultation activity. Depending upon the underlying ideology she suggested three primary consultant roles emerge leading to different activities. The consultant activity is not however confined to one domain as secondary aspects of each role utilize skills found in other systems. This demonstrates that the systems

Table 1: Consultation Models and Roles

Ideological System of consultation	Dominant goals	Consultant roles	
		Primary	Secondary
1. Human development	Personal growth and development	Joint problem solver	Information expert Advocate
2. Scientific–technological	Technical information expertise	Information expert	Joint problem solver Advocate
3. Social/political	Social and political goals	Advocate	Information expert Joint problem solver

themselves are not mutually exclusive. Table 1 presents this way of characterizing the roles consultants can play.

It can be seen that the consultant role closest to the domain of counselling is the human development consultation where the consultant operates in a joint problem-solving mode. Here the client is assisted towards personal goals in relation to an identified problem or system of problems. Similar to the 'therapeutic' context it conveys the balance of the relationship for all that takes place between client and consultant. It also identifies how the provision of technical advice or knowledge is secondary to the process. However, as one might expect, there are differences in emphasis and defining characteristics when the consultation process is completely located within the personal service/counselling context. Again this is best illustrated by an example from the comparison with counselling. In counselling it is often the case that the provision of technical information and advice is implicitly communicated by the counsellor's practice. This occurs via the attention to theoretically relevant material which gradually informs the client of the expected and desirable perspective on their problem. In contrast the consultant is uninterested in client conversion and more genuinely is focused upon the client achieving an elaboration of their 'story', which in itself allows the identification of potential options available for advancing the client perspective and position.

In order to advance this argument a summary comparison between counselling and consultation is presented in Table 2.

In terms of our approach the consultation allows the consultant and the client to proceed, if desired by the client, to another form of relationship, and this could well include a counselling relationship. The movement

Table 2: Consultation and Counselling Compared

Consultation	Counselling
Process initiated and owned by the client, i.e. client determines agenda, goals, end-point	Process initiated by client but ownership is divided between the counsellor and the client
Relationship established to jointly problem solve and receive professional opinion and possibly advice	Relationship established to pursue goals of client change based upon counsellor's theoretical perspective
Symmetrical relationship between consultant and client; equal but different roles	Complementary relationship with counsellor in expert role and client in a dependent role
A process of information exchange which seeks to achieve a common view of the client's situation	A process of information exchange which seeks to elaborate the client's framework and possibly apply a theoretical perspective from the counsellor
A process supported and characterized by the professional's empathic, non-judgemental responses	A process supported and characterized by the professional's empathic, non-judgemental responses
Consultant explains their professional remit and the service they can provide	Counsellors more likely to assume the client has chosen counselling and the need for explanation of professional remit or alternatives is not explored
Consultation focus is upon the client's focal concern as they describe it	Counselling focus and concern is upon the cause of difficulties and the development of solutions
Consultation is always time limited and has an end-phase which is marked by the giving of a public statement of the client's situation and possible courses of action that follow	Counselling is open-ended
The consultation is concluded when the opinion has been given and discussed	Counselling is concluded in various different ways but ideally when the client believes maximum change has occurred
The aim of consultation is to offer involvement in a process and an opinion which will assist the client in making their next decision about their difficulty	The aim of counselling is to promote client change which is perceived as beneficial by the counsellor and client
The consultant perceives the client as being in some active process *vis à vis* his/her problem. The consultation arises out of the client's action plan	The counsellor perceives the client as being stuck in respect of their problem. Counselling arises out of the absence of an action plan
Emphasis in consultation is upon understanding the client's plans and ideas about their difficulty and how they anticipate the consultant assisting them	The counselling relationship is preoccupied with developing and maintaining the client's motivation to change
Consultant remains theoretically flexible in respect of the client's story and view of their problem	Counsellor tends to offer one theoretical view of the client's position and seeks to persuade the client to accept their view of things

from consultant relationship to a relationship of counselling may be facilitated by the consultation process. It should be noted that movement in the opposite direction is extremely problematic if not impossible and may be argued to be another important reason for deferring counselling until the client is in a position to make a more informed choice. Throughout the consultation process primary responsibility for the relationship's direction and progress remains with the client. They set the agenda and remain entirely free to accept or reject some or all of the options offered by the consultant. The consultant's primary professional responsibility is to meet the client's expectations, offer technical information and advice as necessary while in their practice they affirm, as well as actually remind the client of, their freedoms and responsibilities.

The consultant is not in the business of motivating a client to change. Rather the emphasis is upon the understanding of what plans the client already brings and in what way the consultant, through their engagement with the client and his/her envisioned plans, can help facilitate the client's purposeful actions in respect of their problem. That is to say the consultant has no preconceptions as to the quality of the client's plan of action (or inaction). Neither does the consultant make any judgement about these plans within of course the bounds of what is acceptable and legal as well as what is deemed professional and ethical.

Although the consultant is not concerned with motivation *per se*, it is not the case that the consultant dismisses opportunities for the client to consider action that could prove beneficial and therapeutic. Rather the consultant will be attentive to the possibilities of facilitating the client in following a personal plan of action that may enhance personal growth. The counsellor's commitment to particular views about what issues are considered beneficial to growth and development would be made clear to the client. To be maximally effective in the consultant's role and therefore maximally useful to the consultee, the consultant must be capable therefore of 'moving' flexibly through various levels of analysis as indicated by the client's own agenda and construction of their problem. Such conceptual flexibility does not require the abandonment of personal therapeutic orientations but rather a capacity to accept and tolerate the potential range of conceptions from individual functioning to systemic levels which may be presented by the clients.

The 'perfect' consultant therefore is quintessentially post modern in their thinking (see The Social Constructionist View of the Counsellor–Client Relationship, p. 116). It is not that they are without their theoretical or therapeutic inclinations but they accept that each way is merely one way of accounting for the phenomena which describe a client's life. The relationship between consultant and client should be less imbalanced in terms of locus of power and decision making than the traditional counsellor–client relationship. Consultation is therefore most securely anchored and defined by its structure, its goal and the balance of the professional–client relationship. Many of the interactions within the consultation process are the same as those that occur in the counselling process. This is not a problem for the distinctions we have made between consultation and counselling. The former is ultimately constructed to achieve different goals (client decision re choice rather than personal change) and the shift in focus and ambition of the professional as consultant (as opposed to counsellor) serves to create and support a more equal relationship of power avoiding covert activity and intent.

THERAPEUTIC CONSULTATION

Within the general framework of consultation there are some elements that our therapeutic consultation model emphasizes:

- In the consultation the consultant is explicit in his/her entry and participation in a collaborative exercise with the clients.
- The focus of the consultation is the client's outlined agenda and aspirations.
- The consultant, through conversation, reflection and questions of the client regarding their story, develops a view of the problem as the client sees it. This jointly elaborated view also includes elements which at an earlier time have been discounted by the client as being a part of and/or contributory to their difficulty. It also includes the client's plans for whether, how and with whom further steps could be taken.
- The consultation is primarily concerned with identifying the areas of significance and importance in the client's view of a solution.
- The consultation enters end-phase when the consultant, based on his/her public understanding of the situation, outlines various options which he/she believes are open to the client, given the view they have of their situation.
- The consultant may include a summary of his/her understanding and the consequential options in a written form.
- The client's considerations and decisions regarding the consultant's understanding and option appraisal conclude the consultation.
- The client is invited to review the outcome of the consultation at a date in the future.
  (The theoretical ideas which are the foundations for this approach are found as a body in Chapter 7.)

The consultant works from the premise that:

1. The client is, in initial contacts, seeking to advance his/her own plans through the service of a professional rather than anticipating the imposition of a professional plan of action on them.
2. The client's expectation of the professional–client relationship in the first contact(s) is the professional's paramount consideration.
3. The client can be helped by a brief contact with a therapeutic professional.

The effect of combining these three ideas is to conclude that all clients, until proven otherwise, are seeking a consultant–consultee relationship with the counsellor. Our intent as consultants is to establish a very clear relationship with our clients such that we are aware of how they view their problem and how the process of involving a professional counsellor is related by the client to the problem's development. The consultation process is one of working with rather than against or over the client's own expressed needs and expectations of us. As consultants we are very definitely attempting to give clients what they want, notwithstanding the fact that we organize the accounts we hear in terms of developmental/systemic ideas. The general aims of the contact are to:

- establish the consultation as part of a developing/dynamic process around the problem;
- establish the client's problem story in a systemic, interactive, developmental framework;
- establish the client's expectations in relation to potential solutions and possible counsellor actions;
- establish a transparent and collaboratively defined relationship of temporary status.

The consultation interview requires the consultant to steer the flow of conversational exchange through broad areas which are likely to appear and disappear, overlap and collide. All these areas will be discussed in later chapters but at present it is necessary to specify the underlying principles that are the foundation of the interview process.

Principles of the Interview Process

These principles of the consultation interview can be divided into two categories:

1. those principles that relate to the *skills* necessary to conduct the interview;
2. those principles which constitute the basic and structuring ground rules of the interview within the overall consultation process.

Skills

The counsellor in effect questions the system of the client so that the information produced will reveal how that system is interconnected and in what ways the problem is contained within its interconnections. The elucidation of the interactive process is to allow the client(s) to become fully aware of how they function within that system. From this awareness an understanding of their own position in that system develops and this increases the possibility of change. Questions are therefore asked in a way that sets client(s) thinking individually and collectively about the implications of their answers. The questions are not designed to reveal 'facts' but to create a chain of reflexive thought in which the client's interconnectedness to their system becomes apparent (see Consultative Interviewing, p. 148). The consultant is asking questions so as to also acquire an understanding of the client and the problem in his/her system. As the consultant constantly feeds back understanding, the clients are able to relate their perceptions to those that are being publicly expressed by the consultant. A mutual understanding therefore develops as the interview progresses. The consultant is faced and indeed wishes to be faced with a situation in which he/she will never completely understand everything that is happening but by fully utilizing his genuine curiosity about how people interact and by posing questions that refer to the implicit rules and conventions of that system, its operation becomes clearer to those who are taking part in the consultation interview. In order to support his natural curiosity, the counsellor utilizes his awareness of the interconnection of individuals in their natural systems, their families, marriage and social groups. This awareness is placed against the template of the tasks, trials and tribulations of the family life cycle that is relevant to the cultural group to which the client(s) belongs (see The Developmental Perspective, p. 128).

The stance of questioning the system can only be contained within the traditional skills of counselling that come under the title 'non-judgmental active listening'. Accurate empathy, non-possessive warmth and genuineness (Rogers, 1967) are the core conditions of this form of counselling. Means and Thorne (1988) have outlined how these conditions can be put into practice with individuals and Street (1994) has outlined the practice with regard to couples and families. Empathy and warmth are typically seen as being demonstrated by the skill of reflection, which in the case of dealing with an interactive system is seen in two forms. Firstly there is *reflection of feeling,* in which the listener communicates his or her understanding of the other's felt experience; it affirms the individual's experience and at the same time intensifies the awareness of it, thus a feeling of authenticity is experienced. The reflection of feeling therefore allows the internal frame of reference of individual clients to be clarified within the context of relationships. *Reflection of interaction* is the second form and this is important in that it permits the counsellor and client(s) to move between internal frames of reference and the interactions that form the context in which individual perspectives arise. The skill of reflecting interaction is the replaying of any sequence of interaction such that all the participants involved would recognize the process as it happens. It is akin to providing a verbal report of a videotape of an interactive process. It is therefore an opportunity for everyone involved in a social episode to engage in a public re-evaluation of it.

In order to maintain a non-judgemental position with the clients, the consultant adopts a position of 'neutrality'. This neutrality does not refer to an emotional non-involvement but to a non-attachment to the processes and outcomes that the clients present. By maintaining a permanent state of curiosity about what may be happening, the consultant can achieve this type of neutrality (Cecchin, 1987) (see Systemic Ideas and Counselling, p. 122). In being wide-ranging in his thoughts about the situation the counsellor entertains a multitude of possible descriptions of one interaction, hence one description does not and cannot become the 'truth'. The consultant is not seeking the best description or the most suitable description but is interested in constructing a description that fits for that time and place and that might be useful for change now and in the future. The more inquiring the consultant is the more the client has the opportunity to reflect on his/her own interactions. The client comes to realize that the counsellor can and does accept any formulation or description as he does not have any commitment to a right or wrong way of doing things. The removal of any judgemental strait-jacket then allows the client to explore the possibilities of his/her own power and abilities in the problem situation faced.

Ground Rules

There are a number of ground rules which cover the consultation process and which are in place so that the process can move ahead in the most appropriate manner.

1. *The client is considered to be a voluntary client,* that is to say he or she is not under legal compulsion to attend and is considered as dealing in a personal way with any social pressures to attend. Each client is deemed to be entering the process of the interview of his or her own free will and may therefore terminate the counselling contract at any point.

2. *Clients are defined by themselves, not by the referrers.* For the consultation to be perceived as being satisfactory to the consumers, only those individuals who consider themselves to be taking part in the process are clients. Potential clients are identified by referrers but such identification does not ascribe clientship. Typically the principal way clients define their status is by their attendance. Should, for example, a referrer request that the consultant see Mr and Mrs Smith and only Mrs Smith attends, then Mrs Smith is client. During the course of the interview the consultant may ask how it came to be that Mr Smith has not come along and in some circumstances may indicate that it would be helpful if he could attend the second consultation session. However, at no time should the consultant request or insist that Mr Smith does attend.

3. The corollary of this second ground rule is that *clients will decide for themselves who will attend the interview.* The consultant works on the basis that any number of people may attend and the relationship between the individuals may be familial, friendly or professional. Thus, depending on the context in which the consultant works, those who can and do attend will be individuals, marital and co-habiting partners, parents and children, grandparents, parents and children, an individual and a good friend, individuals with work colleagues, individuals with a professional person, a family and a professional person etc. The list is endless.

4. As clients are defined solely by their attendance, *each person who does attend is treated with respect, fairness and equality.* This is done in a manner appropriate to their age and relationship to what has been defined as the presenting problem. Not everybody needs to be treated in exactly the same way. Different ethnic groups may require the meeting of certain conventions when met as a family. Similarly, should a fellow professional attend with an individual 'client' the type of question of the professional may of necessity be of a more technical nature than those directed toward the individual. Sometimes the professional may also be requested to leave an interview when particular material is being dealt with.

5. *When the behaviour of children constitutes the referred problem, the clients are considered to be those adults who assume the parental responsibility for bringing the child to the interview.* Typically this will be one or both parents, though on occasions grandparents may be the adults

concerned and therapeutic consultations can certainly take place with foster parents and care workers. During the interview the children should be communicated with in a manner appropriate to their age and inclination. Younger children tend to play with toys whilst older children frequently wish to sit, listen and take part (see Dowling 1993). Sometimes parents wish to discuss some aspect of their family situation out of the hearing of the children and parents can be seen separately under these conditions.

6. *Consultation only takes place through the interview process.* The consultation is wholly based on the information generated in the interview. Extra-sessional communications with the consultant are discouraged as the material to be discussed needs to be available to all those who attend the interview. If someone cannot/will not attend and they believe that they have a point of view which needs expressing or some information which could be helpful then they should be encouraged to write down their views so that it can be dealt with publicly in the interview.

7. *As far as possible the consultant explains his/her actions* In particular this may involve providing an explanation for asking questions along a particular theme. Here the aim is to make the consultant's activity as 'transparent' as possible so that the clients are informed and aware of all that is taking place and are hence contributing to the consultant's final statements.

8. *The consultant should adopt a flexible approach to the themes in the interview.* In the chapters to follow a step-by-step approach is given of how the information-exchange process may be facilitated. It is not recommended that this approach be adopted in a rigid fashion. The interview will ebb and flow and certain issues will be easier to follow at certain times. The consultant needs to deal flexibly with the 'story' as it emerges so that the clients' predominant experience is a sense of natural conversational flow which occurs with good interviewing. Should the consultant feel a need to return to an issue or begin another topic, this can readily be done at some pause in the interview merely by telling the client that the consultant would be interested to hear about a particular topic.

SUITABILITY AND THE THERAPEUTIC
CONSULTATION APPROACH

It is the convention in books which introduce a new way of working to provide a review of the client characteristics, types of problem or client circumstances which indicate or contraindicate the use of the approach. It is a convention which causes us a small dilemma since our idea of a therapeutic consultation and the relationship which follows from it tend to debar very few clients or types of problems. This is because the emphasis of the relationship is fully maintained on the consultative nature of the contact. The emphasis on 'consultation' alters the relationship between client and professional in a distinctive and, as we argue, in a more fruitful and liberating way. Of probably greater significance in the assessment of suitability is the professional's work context, which we will review in a moment.

Client Characteristics

Having the goal of constructing a consultative relationship means that we can begin by identifying the features or qualities of client which need to be present for a genuine consultation to occur. It is our view that to participate in a therapeutic consultation the consultee must be in a position to:

- recognize they have a problem or difficulty which they wish to talk about;
- give a reasonably coherent (though not necessarily sophisticated) account of their difficulty and their more general situation;
- seek the consultation voluntarily;
- reflect upon their situation and the ideas which emerge out of the consultation process;
- form a reasonable, communicating relationship with the professional almost immediately because of the very brief nature of the contact.

It will be seen that these requirements automatically exclude few people and that most of the contraindications which logically follow from them could equally apply to therapeutic and brief approaches generally rather than being peculiar to this approach. Therefore the principal characteristics of clients which would exclude them from the approach can be described as follows:

1. The legally or otherwise compelled client is not suitable for a consultative approach, because it is the referrer and not the attending individual who is the 'true' consultee.
2. The brevity of the approach means that individuals who are unable to enter and communicate in the relationship almost immediately, perhaps for reasons of debilitating anxiety, severe distrust, etc. are unlikely to be suitable for this approach.
3. The capacity and space to reflect upon ideas from the consultation makes some demand upon intellectual capacity but more importantly

requires the client's situation to be non-critical or otherwise in need of instant action. Thus individuals perceived as being at risk of harming themselves or others are unlikely to be suitable. In addition, however, individuals who feel highly agitated and are unable to resist the need to act may not be able to participate in or make use of the consultation.

4. The broadest and probably clearest contraindication relates to the need for the client to be of sufficient intellectual capacity and steadiness to offer a coherent account of their difficulty and to understand the purpose of the relationship being offered to them. This requirement will tend to exclude the very young, those with a learning disability and those suffering from a severe and current mental disturbance.

Characteristics of the Work Context

Although there appear to be few client characteristics which would be automatic contraindications for this approach there are two major contextual features of the professional's work setting which would make a therapeutic consultative approach unsuitable.

1. We have already referred to the need for the client's status in the consultation to be voluntary. A central idea in the therapeutic consultation is that contact with the counselling professional is *decided* upon by the client (even if the original idea is not theirs and even if others have encouraged them to attend) as part of their continuous effort to resolve personal discomfort. When then the professional is working in a setting where clients are compelled to attend, the professional–client contact does not emerge out of the client's own process of decision-making. Furthermore a consultation in such circumstances can only genuinely occur between the professional and the referrer. Thus, for example, professionals such as probation officers, social workers, and personnel staff will frequently find themselves offering a service to people who are not in circumstances which allow them to be free to leave the relationship or free to act upon or ignore ideas which may arise. A therapeutic consultation approach is not appropiate in working contexts such as these though of course a different kind of therapeutic relationship may be possible.

It is possible for the professional to apply a simple 'test' to establish whether the context would allow a therapeutic consultation to occur, *can the client freely choose to end the relationship with the counselling professional at any time and without reference to the referrer?*

2. The therapeutic consultation approach is also invalidated by the work context when the relationship between the client and the counselling professional is required to achieve 'goals' of a specific or even of a general kind. Goals in this sense may merely refer to an expectation that the contact will *change* the client's behaviour. Clearly expectations of this sort may have been 'established' with the client's interests in mind, rather than say with the third party's (the person who did the 'establishing') interests in mind. Whatever their origin or purpose the presence and influence of such external goals upon the client–professional relationship is to move it into an arena which is not a necessary part of the therapeutic consultation.

Again it is possible for the professional to apply a 'test' to decide whether the context will allow a genuine consultation to occur: *within ethical and professional limits is any client choice, including deciding to make no change, acceptable?*

In this introductory chapter we have attempted to set out the principles on which our approach is based. The following chapters outline in detail the clinical application of these principles when they are put into operation.

2

THE PRESENTING
PROBLEM

The overall aims of the consultation interview are for the consultant to establish with the client:

1. The process that has led to their meeting; this will primarily involve a discussion about the route by which the client was referred.
2. The client's description of the problem.
3. The client's understanding of how others perceive the problem.
4. The solutions that have been attempted and suggested.
5. The interactions that occur around the problem. This involves a discussion of the day-to-day context in which the clients' problem is embedded.
6. The links between the interactive sequence and the client's historical account.
7. The meaning the clients give to the problem and ideology they have about the problem.
8. The expectations the clients have of the consultant and the consultation process.

Aims 1–6 will be discussed in this chapter, and the following chapters will address aims 7 and 8.

THE PROCESS THAT LED TO THE CONSULTATION

● How come we are meeting?

Problems are not in the sole ownership of one person. They are the product of an interactive system and it will be the system that identifies the existence of a problem and labels its presence. When this happens there is then some element of the system that believes that by requesting that a consultant/counsellor/therapist become involved, a solution to the difficulty will more easily be found. This action also involves the problem as being 'passed' to another setting away from the original one. Although this occurs the consultant views the process of referral as an invitation to become a part of the client system and hence to play a role within its functioning. The client is not leaving one system to be sorted out by another – on the contrary the consultant is joining the system to offer his/her own personal contribution to the system's problem-solving process. Some examples will outline this perspective.

> A married man, Mr Hooper, works in a managerial position and begins a relationship with a female colleague; some members of the work team find the situation difficult to deal with and believe it is affecting their efficiency. The matter comes to the attention of the personnel officer who discusses it with the man in question and from this discussion they agree that the man will see a counsellor from the employee assistance programme.

In a situation of this sort there are a number of possible problems that the man could take as a client to the counsellor. There is the problem between himself and his wife that may have led to his new relationship; there is the problem of conducting such a relationship whilst still married; there is the problem of having an intimate (and perhaps clandestine) relationship with a colleague; there is the problem of dealing with other colleagues in regard to the relationship and finally, there is the problem of considering the evaluation the employers are making of the situation. Although all these difficulties are very closely linked, their relative importance to the client will be determined initially by the nature of the interactions that occurred at the time the problem was identified as requiring outside help. In this instance one can imagine the personnel officer saying, 'This is not a good situation to be in. It does need sorting out. Perhaps you need to think about you and your marriage' which is a very different scenario from saying 'We're worried about the efficacy of the work group. This is not helping your career. You need to get it sorted.' Clearly the nature of this discussion between client and the referring personnel officer will significantly affect the manner in which the client will perceive and present the problem to the consultant in the initial interview.

Let us take another example:

> Within a family Mr Dean works long hours and Mrs Dean has the responsibility for the child-care of Jamie their five-year-old son. She struggles with the lad as he does not always do as he is told. She reports this to her husband but he only replies in the 'boys will be boys' mode. One day the family visit the paternal grandparents and the boy misbehaves. The grandmother Mrs Zeta Dean says to her son that she is concerned about the lad

and perhaps 'something should be done'. On arriving home Mr Dean makes an appointment at the family doctor's for the boy which the mother keeps with the boy and the doctor refers the mother and son to a counsellor.

Here we can see how a number of different elements intertwine to make up the overall problem. We can be curious about the operation of some of these elements. Is the mother's greatest difficulty managing the boy or coping with her husband's lack of support? What role does the paternal grandmother's interventions have in the family and how central are they in the desire for change? Such themes cannot be addressed by the consultant unless the process by which the client arrived in the office is fully understood.

In essence the consultant needs to ask questions about such processes so that a link can be established between the consultation itself and what has gone on before. There is a benefit for the client to clearly appreciate that the consultation flows out of the system of interaction that the client naturally inhabits. The consultation is not separate or different from how the client has been discussing and considering the problem with others. Consultation is an activity that is to be seen as a natural part of the client's consideration of the problem. To make this link explicit from the onset, the consultant seeks to identify all those individuals in the client's world who play a role in the 'operation' of the problem. It is important therefore that such people are identified *in terms of their interaction and role* in the referral process as early as possible.

The consultant therefore assists the client to define the boundary around those individuals on whom the consultation will impinge and by this means places the problem within the interactive system in which it occurs. The focus on the 'referral' process additionally serves to clarify who labelled the problem as a problem as this will later allow for some flexibility in agreeing with the client what they may regard as part of the 'problem'. Addressing the issue in this manner therefore also implicitly includes within that boundary the themes and meanings that will emerge later from the client's own presentation of the difficulty. From the outset the client is introduced to the possibility of developing his/her own systemic awareness of their context (see Systemic Ideas and Counselling, p. 122).

Defining the problem boundary also involves placing the consultant within the system dealing with the problem. By being as clear and as public as possible about the consultant's position it then becomes easier to define what the consultant will do as a *part* of the system, how to act and importantly the point at which to step out of the system as an active participant. The first step in framing a public role within the client's system is to declare all that is known at the commencement of the interview. Within the realms of this 'prior' knowledge there are three common scenarios.

1. The only contact has been with the client via telephone or letter and therefore everything is known.
2. The contact has been with a third party, usually another professional, who has written a letter of referral or made a telephone call.
3. A client or referrer has made contact with the consultant and then some other person, be it another professional, or a family member has attempted to communicate with the consultant.

In the case of the latter two possibilities the consultant will have some knowledge about the situation that has been provided by a third party. The consultant needs to be open about who has communicated with whom about the client and what has been said. The aim is that there should be no secrets at all, in order to allow the client to feel in control of the process that is occurring. The only proviso to this situation is that some third parties will communicate information in a prejudiced and judgemental manner and it is certainly not helpful to pass on such expressed attitudes to the client. The content of third party information should be shared in as neutral a manner as possible with just the 'factual' elements being communicated with the clear message being that this information has not set up any preconditions or preformulations.

In the two examples above the consultant may have said the following:

To the gentleman, Mr Hooper:

> 'The EAP office rang me asking that I arrange to see you. All I know is that there seems to be a relationship problem which involves you, a female colleague and the rest of your work group. That's all I know.'

To Mr & Mrs Dean:

> 'Your GP wrote asking me to send you an appointment. He told me that you have been finding Jamie's behaviour difficult. Dr Jones also wondered how you were sharing out the tasks of looking after the boy. After I sent the appointment to you, Mr Dean, your mother rang and I think she wanted to talk to me about the problem. I told her that I couldn't do that but she should discuss it with you and your wife and that together you would then decide who needed to come to the first appointment.'

Following from these statements the consultant can ask some questions that address the issues so far discussed.

- It would be helpful if I know how we come to be meeting. Perhaps you can tell me how it came about?
- Who suggested you should come to see me?
- How did you come to be talking to that person?
- Who else did you talk to before you spoke to that person?
- Who was the first person who thought that what was happening was a problem?
- When was that?
- How did that person tell you?
- Was there anybody else who thought you should see me?
- Who else knows you have come to see me?
- What did the person who referred you say was the reason he was referring you?

In this phase of the interview the consultant acquires information that identifies the time when the problem was first labelled a problem and establishes the interactive pathway of who spoke to whom, ending with the client and consultant talking about the problem.

In the first example, the consultant established that Mr Hooper became concerned with his own situation a short while after he started his relationship with his colleague, Ms King. He had not discussed matters with his wife and he believed she knew nothing about what was happening. He had talked to a friend of his from another city who had suggested that he go to 'Marriage guidance'. A work colleague had raised the issue with him, telling him that it was causing some difficulties in the work group, which he knew about. He had discussed the matter with his girlfriend but it was now all they ever talked about and nothing seemed resolved. The personnel manager had called him in and they had discussed the situation more from the point of view that it was making matters difficult at work. It was the personnel manager who had suggested referral to the EAP. Mr Hooper had told Ms King about this referral but she was unaware that an appointment had been made.

In the second example, Mr and Mrs Dean arrived together. Mrs Dean reported that she knew she had more of a problem with Jamie when she went back to work 9 months ago. She hadn't discussed it with anyone except her husband who didn't think there was a problem. Mr Dean agreed with this. A friend had mentioned to Mrs Dean that she thought Jamie was unruly but she had not known how to respond to this. The family visited the paternal grandparents about once a fortnight and Jamie was usually very difficult there. Mr Dean's mother said something to him about the boy's behaviour when Mrs Dean was not in the room but then they all discussed the problem. Mr Dean said he felt embarrassed that it had happened this way. Almost immediately Mr Dean rang the family doctor for an appointment and the soonest one offered meant that he could not attend and his wife saw the doctor alone. The doctor had said that he thought the counsellor would be the best person to see and he had made the referral.

OBTAINING THE CLIENT'S DESCRIPTION OF THE PROBLEM

- Can you tell me about the problem that led to you coming to see me?
- From your perspective, what is the problem all about?
- When did situation *A* happen in relation to situation *B*? I need to get it right about the timing of these things.

Before the client actually meets the consultant the former will have constructed an idea of how the contact will progress. Undoubtedly the clearest element of this will be how he/she is prepared to tell the consultant about the problem. Clients will have rehearsed what they intend saying about the difficulty. Some clients will have done this in some 'internal' way, others may have practised what they will say with family or friends and some arrive at the interview with an *aide-mémoire* to ensure they cover all the points they need to. It is important for the process of the consultation that the client feels that he/she said all they had planned. Consultation itself takes the description from the client and then via the questioning stance expands on the outline and understanding of the problem. The client's initial description therefore constitutes the foundation on which the rest of the client's story is jointly constructed with the consultant. The consultant therefore needs to allow the client space in which to present this prepared material.

Even though the client is given this space, the consultant does not simply sit back and wait until he/she runs out of steam. The skills the consultant uses include the micro-skills of counselling such as minimal encouragers to talk, paraphrasing, simple clarifying questions and ensuring that the time sequence of events is clear. The last skill is particularly important as a consultant will be aiming to assist the client in describing the problem as occurring within a particular sequence of events and that series of events as being placed within the developing general 'life story' of the client. Consultants and clients benefit from seeing the difficulty as being part and parcel of 'normal' life events and this is facilitated by ensuring that the time sequence of when and what happened is clear. The consultant also uses these skills in order that he is in some way 'structuring' the session from the outset. Research work has shown that clients benefit and expect counsellors to give the session some direction and purpose. For example Gurman *et al.* (1985) concluded that in initial sessions an interviewing style of providing little structure and of confronting affective material can be reliably associated with an observed deterioration in terms of outcome. There do however appear to be some gender differences in client perceptions and preferences of interviewing styles, for Brannen and Collard (1982) found that men were less satisfied than women with an non-directive style, having a preference for more structure. In terms of the consultation interview structuring of this nature is introduced by the consultant seeking clarity on the timing of the events clients describe. From the outset clients are provided with the notion that the problem is being dealt with in temporal terms and is seen therefore as being located within the client's life story. Structure is therefore provided by the organization of the client's story.

This is also the phase of the interview when the consultant begins to tune into the words the client uses to describe events and experiences. Clients' verbal descriptions contain their experience of the problem but at this stage before there has been any reflection on these experiences such words are only the reference point that the client uses in order to organize his/her own thoughts about the difficulties. Words have not as yet come to represent interpersonally negotiated labels of experience and meaning. The client and consultant will evolve this level of shared understanding as their interaction develops through the interview. Therefore for the initial description of the problem the consultant uses the client's nomenclature.

Giving Feedback

The consultation process builds up through the presentation of feedback on what the client tells the consultant. The first major occurrence of when the client becomes truly aware of this process is when the consultant feeds back, in as straightforward a way as possible, the client's initial description of the problem. It is as if the consultant informs the client, 'I ask a few questions, you answer them and then I make sure I have got it right by telling you what you told me.' This first occurrence is when the client can begin to appreciate that his/her account will be given full attention through the listening process and what follows in the session will then be based on the agreed understanding of the client's account. To put it another way the client should experience at this point the 'client-centredness' of the process. Consultants should remember at this point that for the majority of clients being attended to in this manner is a very novel experience and probably does not match any other interaction with which they are familiar. It is for this reason that the reflections offered to the client are simple, straightforward and frequently no more than a plain restatement.

Let us return to our examples.

> Mr Hooper reported that he thought the difficulty was that his colleagues at work found it hard to deal with the fact of his relationship with a younger woman in the office. He thought they were being a bit moral about it. He thought the problems at work were different from the problems with his marriage and his relationship. He really wished to keep the two separate. The relationship had started some six months previously and he knew that some of it was to do with him not being happy in his marriage. He was aware that this type of relationship was called 'an affair' but for him that word did not apply. His work colleagues had become aware of the relationship some four months ago and he thought that the women in the office were being particularly negative about it. Although he thought that he was in a bit of a mess with his personal relationships he thought that he should be able to work it out in his own way.

From this description the consultant noted that the problem in work was presented as the primary difficulty. Undefined words of apparent significance which could be explored later were 'moral', 'negative', 'a bit of a mess' and 'his own way'. The feelings associated with calling the relationship an affair may also be important to discuss.

> In the case of Mr and Mrs Dean with their son Jamie, Mrs Dean reported that since she had returned to work some nine months ago she had found Jamie more of a handful. She had wondered whether James resented her not being there for him. She did not understand why her husband had played down the problems she was having with James. Mr Dean thought that Jamie was being a typical boy and that Mrs Dean, as a typical mother, was finding this rather difficult. Mr Dean said he knew there was a difference in the way things had to be since his wife had gone back to work but he did not know what should be done about it. Mrs Dean thought that her husband only really did things when his mother told him to and she felt upset that it had taken her comment to prompt action about the problem.

From this description the consultant noted that more attention was paid by Mrs Dean to her husband's reactions than to the actual behaviour of the boy. The mother-in-law's intervention was seen by both as being more a reflection on the husband's behaviour as opposed to indicating any possible 'mother-in-law interference'. Undefined words which could be explored later included 'resented', 'not being there', 'a handful', '(husband's) contribution', 'typical boy' and mother's 'upset'.

In some situations a number of family members attend the session and when the request to outline the problem is made the family 'spokesperson' provides the account. The spokesperson is either someone who has assumed this general role or sometimes the family's internal dynamic around the problem has 'elected' a particular person. At this stage the consultant should accept this person as spokesperson as to launch too early into ensuring that everyone has their say will undoubtedly break important family rules that at present are unknown. The consultation process is not a style of intervention in which family rules are discerned and then new interactions introduced to encourage the creation of different family interaction; the consultation process rests throughout on the acceptance of things as they are presented.

In some situations the other family members remain quiet until the spokesperson has completed the account and when this occurs the consultant then merely has the job of asking follow-on questions:

- Is that how you see it?
- Do you want to add anything to that?

In other situations the spokesperson may be interrupted by other family members and here the consultant needs to demonstrate an ability to structure and organize contributions so that everyone has their say. Each account is given attention and respect whilst other individuals are assured they will be given an opportunity to speak and their account will receive the same attention and respect. It is obviously far simpler to provide a verbal feedback of one person's account but when more than one person offers an account and when, as is very likely, those accounts differ, then the consultant is required to demonstrate some other skills. This is best illustrated by an example and let us suppose that on interview Mrs Dean began by complaining about the critical way her husband spoke to her about even the most mundane household activity. Mr Dean might interrupt with his own version of events, perhaps feeling that his wife was discounting him and his views. The couple could well end up arguing about 'what actually happened'. In order to deal with this the consultant would begin by saying 'I find it very difficult to follow things when they're discussed in very general terms. You know what's going on but it would help me if we could discuss a specific incident and then I can hear both your views in turn'. The couple could then in turn be asked to give their version on one specific incident. The consultant would offer feedback on the argument by saying 'Mrs Dean, you saw the incident as being about . . . and Mr Dean, you saw the incident as being about . . .'. If the couple agree with this report the consultant can proceed to the next phase of the interview.

The above example demonstrates one of the defining skills of an interactive approach, namely the ability to paraphrase and summarize statements made by two people. In the situation of interviewing couples and families this will be important throughout. It should be noted that in these early phases of the interview the consultant does not make any attempt to draw any conclusion on relationship between the two accounts: does not say 'you disagree' or 'your view is very different' or 'you appear to be in conflict about this'. These may be relevant comments later as the process unfolds but again at this stage it could easily undermine those processes that keep the consultation brief.

The problem as defined by the client is now the focal point around which the remainder of the session is organized. It is the issue or theme that the consultant will use as the reference point for all future discussion. As the consultant does this it may well be that the client's definition of the problem will change and this will emerge as the consultant clarifies points as the interview progresses. The problem as outlined initially is not accepted as the final once and for all problem. The consultant has to implicitly give the message to clients, 'This is how I understand it but it could of course change.' Even though the content of the problem may change, the fact that there is a problem does not. A problem is required for there to be a focus. In this sense the consultation interview is problem-orientated.

OBTAINING THE CLIENT'S UNDERSTANDING OF HOW OTHERS PERCEIVE THE PROBLEM

A paradoxical element of any client's attendance for consultation is that at one and the same time the client attends in his/her own right and also as a representative of the systems to which he/she belongs. In essence he/she is a representative of the referral system and the family system (though in one of the examples we are developing Mr Hooper is also a representative of his work system). The client therefore needs to be allowed to experience her/himself as an independent autonomous person on the one hand who is interdependent and integrated into a social group on the other. However, because every behaviour is simultaneously a communication to others as well as being an expression of being a person there is a strong tendency to emphasize the latter and categorize our experience as being solely expressions of the self (see Systemic Ideas and Counselling, p. 122). The consultation process has as its goal the attempt to have individuals become aware of their own activity in the systems to which they belong. Significantly, therefore, the point at which the consultant begins to leave the client's rehearsed contribution to the interview is when the issue of other people's perceptions are raised. This is the point at which the consultant and the client begin to construct the social framework that exists around a problem.

The consultant will have already identified those other individuals that are linked to the client and to the problem. Having made a mental list of these people, the consultant wishes to establish the nature of their relationship to the client *via the problem*. The focus of the discussion is on the way clients relate to others when the topic or issue is the problem. The consultant therefore does not, for example in the case of Mrs Dean, begin to ask questions about how she experiences her relationship with her mother-in-law. The questions will concern how her mother-in-law interacts with her with reference to the problematic behaviour of Jamie. Although Mrs Dean may well begin to outline how she gets on in a general way with her mother-in-law, the consultant will be clear to the client that the value of this information is to understand more about the problem-focused relationship. ('So generally your mother-in-law doesn't say much to you, even though you wouldn't mind if she did and I guess that it means she hasn't said much to you about this difficulty?') The consultant should not deal with this aspect of the interview in a rigid manner in focusing only on the specific, but it needs to be recognized that at this stage the consultant wants to establish a very clear picture of the specific. This will make it easier later in the process when suggestions and opinions are offered as the consultant can comment on the way the specific problem may be linked to the general. To begin this inclusion of others into the individual client's psychological field, the consultant asks

- How would person A describe this problem if they had come to see me today?

It should be noted that this question focuses on the description of the problem. It implies that there can be a variety of descriptions, descriptions which in some potential way all could be seen as being of equal standing – but the fact that the client is the client makes his/her description the primary one. The question also clearly gives the message that other people could, in some way, communicate with the consultant. This carries an implication that the consultant can exist in relation to the system and not just in relation to the person sitting in front of them. The consultant is also doing this to begin the process of having 'personhood'

in the process, i.e. that the consultant can and does exist as an autonomous person in the system of consultation. The linking of 'others' to
the consultant even in this hypothetical way does begin to create for the
client the fact that the consultant has the possibility of being an 'other' in
the system.

When undertaking this section of the interview, the consultant needs to
note the extent to which the same words and labels are used and the
extent that they vary. It may be worth while checking out that the same
words mean the same thing. 'When you say your mother would be upset,
do you mean "upset" in the same way as when you referred to yourself?'

The element of the question, '. . . if they had come to see me today?' is
also useful in that it allows the client and the consultant to consider the
other people in the system in terms of their prospective status as clients.
Sometimes others in the system will clearly have a view that the problem is one that requires the intervention of an outsider; some will have a
view that it is a problem but that it can be dealt with by individuals
and/or the system itself and others will not see the problem as a problem. That each person is identified as having a perspective that is potentially of the same importance as everyone else's begins to establish a
framework in which the problem will be seen as existing within the
differing and conflicting perspectives of the system itself. The problem
belongs to the system, not to the relationship between the client and the
consultant.

> In the examples we are following Mrs Dean thought that her mother-in-law
> saw the problem as being that she, Mrs Dean, had taken a lot on and that Mr
> Dean was not doing the right things with the lad. Mr Dean thought that his
> mother saw the problem as being so bad as she did because she herself was
> struggling to look after Jamie during the daytime. They both thought that
> their family doctor did not really have an interest in their difficulty.
>
> Mr Hooper believed that Ms King thought that none of what was occurring
> was the concern of anybody else. In fact he thought that she did not see
> there was a problem at all. Mr Hooper believed that the personnel officer
> wanted a quiet work place and that Mr Hooper should sort out his private
> affairs.

OBTAINING AN OUTLINE OF THE ATTEMPTED
AND SUGGESTED SOLUTIONS

A problem is by definition something that requires a solution and most
people will seek a consultation with a professional person when the solutions they apply do not appear to work. The solutions that exist in a

system at any time may include all those previously *attempted*, i.e. those that the client readily recognizes as having been tried and all those previously *suggested*, i.e. those that the client is aware have been proposed but which for some reason were considered invalid or impractical.

Attempted solutions:

- 'What have you attempted to do in the past to get rid of this problem? What do you do now when the problem emerges?'

Watzlawick *et al.* (1974) have argued that the principal difficulty is not the original problem but the consistent application of a solution that is not working. Many people consider that at the point of consultation they are not attempting any solution and they may give the impression that they are in some resigned way just accepting the problem. In actuality, whenever the problem emerges the client will be attempting to do something about it simply by responding as they do, e.g. complaining that a husband does not help enough. It is the repeated application of this pattern of response that Watzlawick and his colleagues perceive as being the central problem. The consultant does not intend to work with this attempted solution but merely seeks by questioning to establish that the client does put some plan into operation but that it does not affect the situation in the way they desire. An example of this type of approach is the following:

> Mrs Dean reported that when Jamie would not obey a command she would repeat it several times, becoming increasingly angry. Sometimes to avoid fuss she would give up and let Jamie 'get away with it'. Sometimes she would end up hitting the boy and sometimes she would send him to his room.

It is helpful if clients perceive themselves as actively dealing with the problem, even though they are not being successful. This questioning reinforces that clients have taken and are taking some active responsibility for the problem.

For some problems the client may have tried different solutions at different times. Mrs Dean, for instance, may have smacked the lad more frequently at some stage but stopped doing it as it didn't seem to produce any results. The consultant needs to ensure that all these solutions are noted and the time sequences of their occurrence so that the notion of the developing story is maintained.

Suggested solutions may be the following:

- As person A is involved in this, what solutions have they suggested that you try?

- As person A is involved in this, what solutions might they suggest?

Some individuals will actively seek the views of others as to how they should deal with a problem. Some people will readily suggest a solution whether they are asked for it or not. Suggested solutions can be viewed by the client in a number of ways.

1. A suggestion which because of it origin must be 'wrong'; the client is then justified to continue with his/her own solution.
2. A solution that has been tried in the past but did not work – the client thereby feeling justified that everything has been tried.
3. A solution which is discounted because it comes from a particular person.
4. A solution which is discounted because the person making the suggestion does not understand the client's position.

In essence, these types of perceptions reveal how the beliefs of one individual (about what another suggests) make a statement about the nature of the relationship between those individuals. At this stage of interview, however, the consultant will be wishing to establish the 'facts' of the system, i.e. who says what. This orientates the client to the boundaries of what is being considered but unless the client volunteers information on why he/she discounts a particular suggestion or believes that it has not worked or cannot work, then all that needs to be acquired at this stage is a list of particular attempted and suggested solutions.

> Mr Hooper and Ms King had initially tried to keep their relationship secret but this proved to be impossible. He had thought of saying something to his colleagues in the work group but the time never seemed right. He had also considered telling somebody higher in management about it but he and Ms King had decided that it was none of their business. Ms King had adopted a strategy of saying that they should just ignore how their work colleagues were dealing with it as everyone needed to have an 'adult' approach about all this. He thought his work colleagues believed he would do best to stop the affair as this was the moral thing to do and would sort out the problem for them. He thought his personnel manager wished him to stop the relationship as things in the office would then return to normal.
>
> Having obtained these views of the primary problem the consultant asked, 'I know that the marital problem is very much a secondary issue for us to consider but how do you think your wife would suggest you dealt with this difficulty?' 'No doubt about it,' replied Mr Hooper, 'she would want me to stop the relationship.'

In the last element of the example above, it can be seen that the consultant frames questions based on the information that has been acquired previously. The client's view is that his primary problem is at work and the marital issue is only a secondary issue and this perspective has been readily accepted by the consultant and is conveyed in the question asked. Mr Hooper could have replied that as it was a secondary issue it was not worth discussing in the interview and that would clearly have established a very important aspect of the boundary around this particular consultation. However, this is not the case in the consultation and therefore at least some aspects of the marital situation are contained within the boundary of the consultation.

In consultations where couples or a number of family members are present, the consultant will need to clarify every person's view of what solutions they each have attempted and this may also involve suggestions they have made to each other. For example if a parent is constantly arguing with a teenager the other parent's attempted solution to the whole problem is to suggest to the teenager not to argue. Discussions about solutions in families therefore reveal who is perceived as being the person who is capable of taking most action to enable the problem to go away. It also needs to be remembered that in family/marital interviewing it is very possible that individuals will begin to disagree about attempted solutions in the session. This happens because conflict in families is typically about ways of doing things differently to avoid something being troublesome. The consultant will need to ensure that he has enough authority to merely sample this conflictual interaction, and then make a note of its nature and occurrence whilst still ensuring all possible solutions have been expressed by family members.

TRACKING THE INTERACTIONS IN WHICH THE CLIENT'S PROBLEM IS EMBEDDED

The next task of the interview continues the shift from a problem as experienced by an individual to one that resides within the functioning of a system. In order for this 'expansion' to occur the consultant helps the client move from a static outline of the problem and its solutions to one in which the problem is appreciated as being linked into a much wider framework of interactions. From the client's initial view the problem being encountered is limited to a particular set of behaviours and interactions in which the sentiments are 'If I or they didn't do such-and-such, there would be no problem'. The client therefore *punctuates* the interaction in which they are taking part within a relatively short timespan. As Mrs Dean says, 'I try talking to my husband and he doesn't listen.' Even if we allow for the shorthand of what actually happens, Mrs Dean says she begins the interaction by speaking to her husband and he ends it by ignoring her. So for Mrs Dean this 'set' of interactions is separated from other 'sets' and in common with all inter-active sets it has a beginning and an ending. Much as with writing a sentence, you start with a capital letter and end with a full stop and punctuating words in this way gives a particular meaning when sepa-rated from the other meanings around it. However, the systems view is that life is just a continual stream of interactions (words) and where one places the beginnings and endings (capital letters or full stops) is ul-timately arbitrary. Each way of punctuating interaction can make sense in its own right and the consultant therefore seeks the broadest possible outline of the interactions around the problem so that the potential for different punctuations becomes possible (see Systemic Ideas and Coun-selling, p. 122). The attempt to do this has the aim of moving the clients from observing only their own perspective in the system to one in which they observe the interactions of others and the perceptions of those others, and hence they move to watching themselves as a third person in the interactive system. To do this the consultant requests the client to select a typical occasion on which the problem occurred and then fol-lows the sequence of interactions including those before the 'beginning' as well as those after the 'end'.

- Let's take an example so you can tell me what happens when the problem is apparent. For example, did it happen yesterday? Tell me what happened.
- That's how it started. Can you tell me what happened before that?
- So that is how it finished. What happened after that?

Mr Hooper reported the previous day's problem as being the funny looks he received from colleagues when he and Ms King went out for lunch. When they returned there was a difficult atmosphere in the office which stopped him from giving them directions about the tasks at hand. The consultant asked what had happened beforehand. Seemingly nothing dif-ferent had occurred. When the consultant asked how it was decided that they would go to lunch on that particular day, Mr Hooper said how he had felt they had been seeing too much of each other so they had agreed on having lunch no more than once a week as well as two evenings at other times. Ms King had felt it important that as matters were public they should do something that did not hide things and Mr Hooper had just gone along with this. The consultant checked by a simple summary. 'So before last week you felt you were seeing too much of Ms King and so you negotiated with her times when you could meet.' On asking about what happened when they returned from lunch Mr Hooper reported that they were a little late back and everybody else was about their jobs. Nobody made any refer-ence to their returning and nobody said 'Hello'. Unusually nobody came to

Mr Hooper with any query and somehow nothing 'broke the ice' which would have allowed Mr Hooper and members of the group to talk to each other again. Ms King just got on with her job and Mr Hooper did not see her talk to the others. He had waited until the following morning to say what he needed to the group. The consultant also asked 'And what happened when you got home?' Mr Hooper said that he felt very miserable about the whole thing, about work and his relationship with Ms King. He felt distant from his wife. She had asked him how his day had gone. He was short with her, they had not had a conversation and the evening continued with little talk 'in the way we do'.

In this section we note that what happened at the workplace was to some extent determined by the negotiation in the relationship. The couple, for example, could have agreed not to meet for lunch because of the difficulties it caused at work. Also the negotiation was precipitated by some concerns that Mr Hooper had about how they were managing the relationship. We find that the interactions in one context, the relationship, is having an effect on the interactions on another, the work group. This pattern is also repeated in that the context called 'work' led to Mr Hooper behaving in such a way that his interactions in the marital context were difficult.

In our example of the Deans, Mrs Dean begins her report by saying that she had had a difficult day at work. She returned home to find her husband there and no chores had been done. Jamie was tired and demanding of attention and the tea needed to be prepared. She found herself trying to do two things and her husband was upstairs. Jamie was refusing to eat his supper and she had to tell him off for throwing his food around. Mr Dean came into the room and made a comment about shouting too much. Mrs Dean felt hurt and just got on preparing tea. Mr Dean left the kitchen again. Mr Dean's report began with saying that he had got home a little before his wife – which was unusual. He was not sure what he should do and so he put the kettle on. His wife came in and did not greet him well and more-or-less ignored him. Again, not knowing what to do he left the room. He went back in the kitchen when he heard his wife shouting at Jamie. He said something about the shouting and Mrs Dean ignored him again so he left the room.

From the consultant's questions he established that Mrs Dean had had a difficult day because the shop in which she works was very busy with not enough staff. They had not discussed what they would have for tea as Mrs Dean 'did it in her head' and Mr Dean did not really know 'how to organize it'. The couple in fact seldom had a discussion about how tea would be prepared and what it would consist of. The consultant also established that it was assumed by both that Mrs Dean would pick up their son from her mother-in-law.

Here is an example of how the consultant, by simply asking questions about what led to what, is implicitly referring to potential alternative ways of behaving. In this sense what appears to be a simple clarifying question ('How did you decide who would pick up your son?') implicitly contains the embedded suggestion that perhaps a discussion could take place and the outcome of this may make a difference to the interactions that follow.

> Having established that no negotiation took place between the couple early in the day or at the point when they saw each other again, the consultant turned the focus of the interview on to what happened in the time following the end of the narration provided by the couple. Their story finished when Mr Dean left the room and Mrs Dean continued seeing to the boy and preparing the meal. Following this Mr Dean continued to feel that he did not know what to do and he just sat watching TV. At one point he went and asked his wife if she wanted him to do anything and he was told 'It's too late now'. After he finished his supper the boy went to his father who played a game with him. The couple did not talk again until they sat down to eat. Mr Dean apologized to his wife but he was not sure what he was apologizing for. They did begin to talk when Mrs Dean told her husband about the boy's difficult behaviour. Mr Dean asked his wife if she wanted him to clear up the dishes from their meal or get James ready for bed and she asked him to get the boy ready for bed. The remainder of the evening they were 'amicable' with each other but they did not really discuss anything in any meaningful way.

In these examples we can see how the consultant has extended the time zone around the problem behaviour such that a more comprehensive and elaborate perspective on what happens becomes available. In the case of Mr and Mrs Dean, however, there is another interactive element that needs to be included and this involves how Mrs Zeta Dean the paternal grandmother becomes involved in the sequence.

> In the example we are pursuing, the consultant asked Mrs Dean whether anything happened when she picked up the boy from her mother-in-law's. Mrs Dean reported that as was usual his grandmother told her that the boy was fine but that he had to be watched because he could not be left without supervision and needed adult firmness. That appeared to be it but the consultant, being curious about the involvement of Mrs Zeta Dean in the referral, wondered how else she might be active within the family system, so he asked Mrs Dean if she discussed matters with her mother-in-law when she left the boy there. The reply to this was that nothing like that happened. In his puzzlement the consultant asked, 'So how does Mrs Zeta Dean find out about how bad things are?' and both parents instantly reported that she telephones them in the evening to make sure that the boy is all right. So this conversation between mother and daughter-in-law went along the lines of Mrs Zeta Dean asking how the boy was when he got home, Mrs Dean would then complain that Mr Dean had done nothing in the home and Mrs Zeta Dean would sympathize with Mrs Dean about the problems she had with father and son.

There is a tendency for us all to concentrate exclusively on our perceptions of the core elements of any interactive sequence. In our reporting of an event everyone will leave out the actions of someone who at that time may appear 'peripheral' but who does play an important role. In order for the consultant to obtain as full a picture as possible, it is necessary to ensure that everyone's activity during this particular time frame is included. Even if someone appears to be sitting there doing nothing it is still valuable to ensure that this element is also included in the overall sequence of events.

In some consultations children will be present and as we have seen in the current example, a major part of the interview process may include talking about their behaviour. A number of authors have specifically addressed the manner in which young children can be approached in family sessions. (Dare and Lindsay, 1979; O'Brien and Loudon, 1985; Dowling, 1993). In general the skills utilized by the consultant in talking to children will follow closely the skills outlined by these family workers. These skills are extensions of good communication skills with children which are a natural part of effective parenting. However, as stressed earlier in the section on ground rules, the consultant's clients in this situation are the parents. Because of their age and developmental capacity it is not possible for children to exercise the individual autonomy necessary to become clients in their own right. Therefore the consultant needs to involve children in the verbal discussions in a way that is appropriate to their age and status. Indeed it is when the focus is on obtaining an interactive overview that the consultant can ask the children the same question as the adults, 'What happened when . . .?' Before this moment in the interview to treat the children in the same way as the adults would have been disrespectful to the generational boundaries of the family. However, when all family members are treated as observers and reporters of family interaction then it is possible for children and adults to be dealt with in a similar fashion. Carpenter and Treacher (1989) note that doing this in this way can serve to expand the focus of the discussion by making available another set of relationships to act as a context for the themes and interactions being discussed. In our example, however, it is considered that James is not able to effectively and meaningfully contribute to the discussion and therefore apart from ensuring that he is appropriately occupied and content in the session the consultant does not directly question him as a full partner in the family process. At various points the consultant will address him in some innocuous way, however. This will keep him as a person present in the interview who, in some appropriate way, is maintained as a cooperative participant even if that only means he is sitting and drawing quietly.

In the whole process of acquiring an interactional perspective, the counsellor will have been using the skill of 'reflection of interaction'. The counsellor slowly tracks through the interactive chain as reported by the clients, being sure that in his replies to them each link in the chain is dealt with so that for himself and for the clients the development of the interactional sequence is well understood. The consultant will repeatedly sequence the interactional account saying, 'Let me see if I'm getting this right; first you did (this) then he did (that), so you did (this) and he did (that)?' It is in the presentation of this larger interactive framework that the client may begin to feel that choices are in existence which initially did not seem to be present. The words used to describe each action are either quite neutral or the words used by the clients themselves. The consultant in effect slows down the speed of the interactions so she and the clients can achieve a full view of it.

Therapeutically, the slowing process also offers to the clients an opportunity to reconsider a series of events that they have grown used to by seeing it in an expanded, slightly distanced and hence novel form. The error to avoid at this juncture is the desire to introduce new frames and perspectives on the interactive sequence hoping to increase the therapeutic effect on the client. To undertake such actions one requires a relationship of a different order with a client, one in which the counsellor/ therapist introduces unilateral elements from their own perspective. The 'consultation alliance' is formed by a close following of the client's perspective alone.

Toward the end of this stage of the interview the consultant should ask whether or not the sequence followed is typical of how the problem presents. The majority of clients quite naturally outline a typical occurrence of the problem. However, for a few there may be major differences between what happened 'yesterday' to what happens 'usually'. This is the second pitfall to avoid for there are clients who will spend more time telling the consultant about the events that made yesterday untypical rather than focus on the typical events. 'Unusual' happenings may mask the more typical interactive sequence. It is important that the consultant be able to acquire for himself and the client a good description of the typical sequence but at the same time be able to relate these events to the fact that it is possible for unusual happenings to interfere with the interactions around the problem.

LINKING THE INTERACTIVE SEQUENCE WITH THE CLIENT'S HISTORICAL ACCOUNT

It is at this stage that the consultant is beginning to get ready to provide the client with a feedback of the 'story' as recounted so far. Many clients will have spontaneously referred to elements of history that relate to the themes already focused on. However, it is useful for the consultant to ensure that all major elements of history have been covered. Street (1994) has outlined how in the counselling process there is a need to link the time frames of historical time; 'before' time; last week; next week and the future. This is necessary as clients with problems often become so focused on present difficulties or past history that they feel there is no prospect of change in the future. The consultant has a different orientation to the client time frames, because of offering major 'feedbacks' at different stages in the process. The consultant considers the past history elements within the stage of the interview that deals with the problem and its interaction. The future aspects of client's time will be dealt with in that stage of the interview after the problem stage. Clients tend to categorize time for themselves into three past periods and two future. The first past period is that of *historical time* – for an intact family this is before the current primary adult relationship developed. In the examples we are following in this chapter this time refers to the time before Mr and Mrs Dean got together. From a general counselling viewpoint this time is noted as it may well contain patterns of relating which dominate the present. In counselling/therapy the strategy is to help clients feel linked to the positive elements of their history but psychologically separated from the negative. The consultation process, however, does not have such an historical perspective. The manner in which it deals with history is in terms of its narrative framework. Therefore historical time only has an importance if it is spontaneously mentioned by clients. In our experience this happens to a limited extent in situations where clients present for consultation with an expectation of understanding and explaining an ongoing problem to themselves. This type of client will be discussed in Chapter 5. A large proportion of clients do not spontaneously report on this time frame. The consultation process focuses on what is happening and how clients understand this for themselves. Therefore time frames distant from those of the immediate period are relevant only in that they provide information on the designated problem in its development.

In terms of time that is distant, the most useful in the consultation is that which can be characterized as *'before' time*. Clients readily refer to a time before the problem emerged. This may be the time before the elderly in-law came to stay, before the husband began a new relationship or before a particular developmental stage was reached. It is interesting that some clients will date the timing of 'before' (a problem existed) as being around some particular event – sometimes minor – a holiday or the car breaking down or sometimes something that was particularly stressful; the dog dying, difficulties at work, a family bereavement. This pivotal event may very often have little bearing on the problem or its later development. It is just the event that is used to punctuate the time 'before' there was a problem and the time that followed. For some people the 'before' time will refer to halcyon days when the individual and family functioned well, others will recognize this period as just being 'without the problem'. The aim of the consultation process is to assist the client in identifying the difference between 'before' time and the present. The consultant is constantly attempting to work in a way which implies the development and hence the continuous change of things through time. If once there was not a problem and then there was then equally a time can be achieved when there no longer is a problem. The consultant is therefore asking the question,

● How did you deal with these types of issues before this problem?

The client then has the opportunity to retrieve the positive qualities of the previous time so that they can be applied to the future. This question also seems to identify the event or series of events that punctuate the 'before' and following time. In being able to 'date' the problem in this way the client then becomes oriented to situations that may need to be reviewed, adapted to or simply adjusted.

> In our examples the consultant asked Mr Hooper 'In terms of finding out what it was like before, I would like to ask what things were like before you began your relationship with Ms King.'
>
> Mr Hooper's report was that he was feeling very stuck and bored in his job and the relationship 'pepped things up'. Also he knew that he and his wife were not getting on well and somehow he had not wanted to do anything about it. He was not sure whether his marriage was affecting his job or his job affecting his marriage.
>
> In regard to the Dean family, both partners spontaneously reported that the pivotal time was when Mrs Dean returned to full-time working; before that time they agreed that Mrs Dean took responsibility for the household chores in a 'typically woman's way'. They also agreed that Mrs Zeta Dean enjoyed seeing her grandson frequently but as she is now having to look after him this was not as often.

The other element of past time the consultant deals with is that which can be identified as *last week*.

● How have things been last week compared to the time before?

This is the period just prior to the session and most likely the emotional tone and atmosphere present at the beginning of the interview will largely be determined by 'last week'. Frequently the whole history of the problem may seem to be defined solely in terms of 'last week'. It is very easy for clients to respond to the recent past as if it were a continuation of how the problem has been for some while. The consultant's questions invite each client to review 'last week' in realistic terms; the problem can be identified as having a change element through time. When the consultant checked out this aspect with Mr Hooper he was able to identify that last week was different because he was now trying to put some kind of limit around his relationship with Ms King.

The First Feedback

We have now arrived at that point in the interview when the consultant will attempt to present in summary form all the information that the clients have imparted. He will do this in the form of a story which seemingly will have a beginning, a middle but as yet no end. The end implicitly is what the client decides to do next. In order to present this feedback the consultant presents the material in a particular order so that the quality of the story is maintained in its 'historical' sense. This is important for when we consider client stories in this way the role of the consultation itself assumes its rightful position of being only a sub-plot. It is only part of the process of the client dealing with this problem. It is not the one and only focus. The client is therefore given an overview of the process that has occurred for him or her. The additional element that the consultant introduces is to cast the obvious features of the client within a simple family developmental life cycle phase (see The Developmental Perspective, p. 128) For example, in the case of Mr Hooper the consultant began by saying 'well obviously you are a forty-four year old man with a wife and family in a responsible position at work.' Nothing else needs to be added to this as Mr Hooper knows perfectly well the experiences of a forty-four year old man with a wife and family and a responsible position at work. The consultant has permission to make such statements (but at present only succinctly) because he has dealt with the problem in its development over time and this does simply describe Mr Hooper's position. Following this identification of the life-cycle position, the consultant should feed back to the client in his own words the story in the following order:

- the 'before' time, including any references spontaneously made about historical time
- the pivotal event that signified the start of the time when the problem existed

- the problem as described generally in its interactive context
- the problem as described by significant others
- the problem as it presented last week with reference to any events as to why it may have been different to that described generally
- the attempted solutions
- the interactive process that led to the client seeing the consultant.

In the case of couples and families the consultant may for each issue have to give feedback on each person's account. The aim is not to present two sides of an argument that need to be judged and resolved but merely to state clearly and neutrally that there are two or more perspectives on the problem and events and these are what they are.

In order to orient the reader with regard to the two examples and to prevent being unduly repetitive, the most salient features of each case will be presented in note form:

- Mr Hooper
  - Mr Hooper is a 44-year-old man. He has a wife and two children.
  - For about 18 months he has been feeling very stuck and fed-up.
  - This feeling has been about work and about his marriage – he is not sure if one is affecting the other.
  - He begins a relationship with a work colleague, Ms King which 'peps things up'.
  - His other work colleagues find this relationship difficult and they seem to view it very morally. The problem somehow stops people at work from talking to each other.
  - His personnel manager views this relationship as interfering with the productivity of the work group and believes it should be kept separate from work.
  - His wife does not know about the relationship.
  - The problem was a little different last week as he tried to limit the amount of contact with Ms King but she wished for them to continue in their 'public' manner.
  - The personnel officer asked to see Mr Hooper and suggested a referral to the employee assistance programme in order for Mr Hooper to sort out things.
- Mr and Mrs Dean
  - Mr and Mrs Dean are a couple in their late twenties. They have one child aged 5 years old (Jamie).
  - Following the birth of Jamie, Mrs Dean remained at home and was a full-time housewife and mother and this situation continued until Jamie was about to start school.

— At this time Mrs Dean returned to full-time work.
— It was decided that the child-care arrangements – picking up Jamie from school etc., would be with the help of Mrs Zeta Dean – the paternal grandmother.
— Mrs Dean senior had always been involved with the family.
— Since beginning full-time work Mrs Dean feels that her husband has not changed his contribution to the family tasks.
— Mr Dean believes his wife has found it all too much since starting full-time work.
— They both agree that since this time Jamie has become difficult.
— The problem is that Jamie wants his own way, in a typical incident Mrs Dean shouts at him, Mr Dean asks if he can help, he is told 'No', Jamie is given in to and Mr and Mrs Dean do not speak to each other.
— Mrs Zeta Dean rings up every day to 'check' on how things are; she says to her daughter-in-law that Jamie is a problem and says that her son is not doing enough.
— Mrs Dean (Senior) told her son that their was a problem that he should sort out and he made an appointment with the family doctor who referred the family on to the consultant.
— Mrs Dean willingly came to the appointment with the consultant. Mr Dean was not sure it would help.

We will now go on to consider the next set of interview aims in the next chapter.

3

PROBLEM MEANING AND IDEOLOGY

When working with clients in a brief therapeutic mode the consultant seeks to implicitly offer a means of categorizing behaviour that is linked to problems. This categorisation is based on the difference between events and beliefs about the events, for although beliefs and behaviours are linked they are still different. In the previous chapter events were dealt with in a way that kept the focus on the interactions between people. This was achieved through the process of constructing a temporal sequence which of necessity placed the events within a traditional narrative context. The next phase of the consultation interview deals with the process of elaborating that sequence of events so that the bare narrative becomes a personalized story, i.e. by including the meaning that the client places on the events they observe, contribute to, and the meaning they give to the actions of others also involved in those events.

It has been suggested that human social advancement has been achieved out of our need to control or understand our world and our experiences in it. In placing psychological order in our world we do not simply organize it but actively construct it. In doing this we therefore become able to deal with future time by predicting how we believe events will unfold. The psychologist George Kelly (Kelly, 1955) suggested human beings act as scientists, they construct a theory of how particular events happen and then use their perception of other life events to verify that theory. The theory then becomes a tool for predicting the future. The central concept of Kelly's view is the construct, which is a belief or ascribed meaning that is applied in the understanding of other people and social situations. The individual develops many constructs which are then linked to other constructs such that a system of thinking, of inter-related constructs, evolves. The system of constructs then shapes and determines how the individual thinks about, and experiences the world (see Dallos, 1991). In any marriage or family it is possible for there to be sufficient overlap of rules about the relationship between one person and another that one can consider there is a family or marital ideology. We use the word ideology to refer to a particular set of constructs which portray these personal values and ideals; not only does it imply an organized body of ideas that reflect the beliefs of someone but it also implies something that reflects the interests of that person. An ideology therefore not only tells us how an individual thinks about a particular situation but it also gives an indication of how that situation will be evaluated in terms of self-preservation, self-gain and the meeting of ideals and values. Ideology therefore points to activities that the individual will pursue in order to maintain their own sense of integrity and these activities can and will be things that involve future planning and the commitment to action (see Personal Construct Theory, p. 143).

In coming to an appreciation of the client's ideology several areas need to be considered.

1. the ideology about the problem;
2. the ideology about the perspective of others;
3. the ideology relevant to future time;
4. the ideology about the consultant;
5. the ideology about the consultation process – testing out solutions.

Within our principles of practice (see Chapter 1) it was stressed that matters need to be dealt with in the conversational flow of the interview. At this stage of the interview it is important that the client feel that his/her recounting of the story is important to the consultant while at the same time becoming aware that the consultant is distinguishing between interactive events and explanations about those events. Clients are helped if they appreciate the difference between 'What happens?' and 'Why do you think that happens?' Some clients tend to focus on the 'why' elements from the onset and it is then necessary to construct a view of the 'what'; other clients begin with the 'what' and need to be encouraged to verbalize their 'why'. Some clients are helped by the consultant distinguishing between 'what' and 'why' for each element of the story so that the whole 'what' and 'why' is built up piece by piece. A few clients give their information in such a straightforward manner that the consultant's questions are rather minimal. Whatever situation obtains the consultant should be wary of giving the client the impression that first we deal with the 'what' which is one thing and then we deal with the 'why' which is another thing altogether. The consultant is aiming to frame a gestalt of the whole situation, some information will come spontaneously from the client and some will come from the consultant asking questions of elaboration and clarification. When dealing with these issues the client should

therefore experience the consultant as simply checking on and obtaining information that is necessary for the consultant to fully understand and appreciate the situation.

Having agreed the sequence of events with the client it is then possible to move on to the questioning about the different meaning of the events. The time sequence of events instructs the direction of the consultant's questioning about explanations. But the consultant does not just limit his questions to eliciting explanations, he also wishes to explore the implication of those explanations. Every explanation carries with it an implication about an action that would change, stop or alter the event under discussion. The implication of any explanation or ideology may contain action that has the potential for being a solution to the problem. Importantly it is the link between explanations and the potential solutions implicitly contained within the client's ideology that the consultant wishes to explore.

The consultant has to ensure that the client does not experience the search for meaning and explanation as being a search for blame. The consultant is offering the client the opportunity to consider his/her position from another perspective and therefore it is important that the consultant create the atmosphere where views and ideas and not just prejudices are being obtained about the issue in hand.

In essence the consultant asks the questions,

- Why do you think this is happening now?
- How do you explain all this to yourself?

It is not unusual for clients to have very firm ideas on why certain events occurred which they can readily articulate but they may not have such a command or even realization about the future action implied by such meaning ascription. In answer to the above question concerning 'Why now?', Mr Hooper may reply that his wife's behaviour resulted in his beginning his relationship with Ms King then the consultant should follow through with a question that identifies some future action that Mrs Hooper could take that would lead Mr Hooper into believing his marriage was functioning more appropriately 'Do you think there is anything your wife could do that would lead you into thinking that things were better?'

- As your explanation involved person X is there anything that person could do to make the situation better?

The link the consultant is making is between the client's views about what has happened in the past to what could happen in the future. In this fashion the consultant is allowing the client to appreciate his responsibility for what he thinks but at the same time he needs to link this with the client's own agency in the system. This then becomes the next link in the chain as the interviewing process moves from description of interaction to exploration of possibilities in the future.

Mrs Hooper paying her husband more attention then becomes a potential solution which Mr Hooper has to evaluate in the context of all the other potential solutions that may arise in the interview. In evaluating this particular solution interactively what is called into question is the action that Mr Hooper could take in order for this potential solution to become activated. In other words 'Mr Hooper what do you think you could do in order for your wife to give you more attention?'

- What could you do that would allow person X to take the action that you consider suitable?

He may consider that spending more time with his wife may produce a difference and so the potential solution becomes a possibility but only if he is able to find more time and only if he wishes to. He, however, may consider that there is nothing he can do that would ensure his wife gives him more attention and therefore no potential solution arises out of his ideology about this aspect of the problem. If indeed this was the case the consultant could provide the feedback that nothing much can be done about the marital relationship because Mr Hooper feels nothing can happen that would change it.

The above example demonstrates the ideology/potential solution sequence in which the consultant elicits an explanation about an event, logically continues with questions about actions that are related to the explanation, particularly questions about future actions that would improve matters, i.e. actions that would prevent the event in the future. Actions that could become potential solutions are then identified and finally actions that the client could take him/herself to guarantee an occurrence of the potential solution are also identified. The steps in this can be outlined as

Explanation
Action that resulted in event
↓
Action that would prevent event in future
↓
Action that could potentially be a solution
↓
Action by client that would ensure one occurrence of potential solution

So in these terms we can summarize Mr Hooper's situation as

Action that resulted in event (the poor marital relationship)	Wife not giving enough attention
	⇓
Action to prevent event	Wife giving more attention
	⇓
Action as potential solution	More attention from wife will lead to better relationship
	⇓
Client's action to ensure occurrence of solution	Spend more time with wife

Here we have identified Mr Hooper's ideology about his relationship with Mrs Hooper and linked this to a potential solution. As was noted above the final evaluation of this solution's viability is Mr Hooper's.

In couples and families there will be two or more explanations for any event and hence two or more sequences that could lead to potential solutions. With the problem behaviour that Jamie Dean presents, Mr Dean may believe that Jamie began to be difficult because his wife went to work whereas Mrs Dean may believe the problem began as her husband has not changed to cope with her going out to work. Their respective ideology/potential solution sequences would therefore be as follows:

Mrs Dean

Action that resulted in event (Jamie's difficult behaviour)	She needs more help because she is now working full-time. Mr Dean has not changed enough to help her
⇓	
Action necessary to prevent event	Mr Dean taking on more household chores
⇓	
Action as potential solution	Mr Dean agreeing to do more and recognizing what has to be done
⇓	
Action by client to ensure one occasion of solution	Tell husband what to do and not do every thing

Mr Dean

Action that resulted in event   Mrs Dean going out to work and
                                                 not being so available to Jamie as
                                                 she is busy

                                    ⇓

Action to prevent event   Mrs Dean not being so fussy about
                                                 cleanliness and all the chores –
                                                 learn to leave it. Spend more time
                                                 with Jamie

                                    ⇓

Action as potential solution   Mrs Dean letting things be

                                    ⇓

Client action to ensure one   Tell Mrs Dean to leave it
occurrence of solution

Immediately one can see that these two ideology sequences are in conflict. Mrs Dean has identified that she should identify chores to her husband and Mr Dean believes he should say 'leave it'. Again the consultant does not wish to enter into the conflict theme at this stage but merely wishes to ensure that it is recognized by all, as later in the process these issues can be explored a little more fully. However, with regard to couples and families, it should be noted that sometimes two people will begin to argue as the conflict between them is made apparent. When this occurs the consultant should take note of the issue that led to the argument, allowing the interaction to occur for long enough for him to identify the interactive elements and then reflect back to the family the interaction that occurred. In the case of the Deans, the consultant may therefore feedback with empathic neutrality, 'Is this how it is at home? Mrs Dean makes a comment about the situation, Mr Dean becomes angry, Mrs Dean becomes angry and then Mr Dean withdraws? That sounds stressful for you both.'

In couples and families it is also more appropriate to go through the ideology/potential solution sequence in full for each individual. This is so that each individual feels they receive 'equal treatment' with regard to their ideology, a situation not so necessary when only one individual is being interviewed as clients soon learn the process and steps can then be skipped.

At this stage in the consultation process action that can be taken by the client only is identified; the consultant does not elaborate on this or take the client into a discussion of the fine tuning of such action. To do more than identify would take the process away from consultation and hence potentially limit the range of behaviour open to the consultant. As the purpose of investigation is to clarify and expand the ideology of the client rather than identify and work with potential solutions, it is to be expected that the vast majority of sequences followed will not identify solutions. To return to Mr Hooper as the example, he could identify his spending more time with his wife as a solution, but suppose that he is unable or unwilling to do this. It cannot be stressed enough that in the consultation process such statements are as important as potential solution statements. The consultant here for example could reflect this as being 'So you believe there is nothing you can do that may help change your wife's behaviour toward you?' This is the 'nothing can be done' end result of this part of the ideology/potential solution sequence. In this sense therefore such a clarification specifies the limits of action that the client believes him or herself to have.

By ranging through all the events and interactive sequences in this way the client is confronted with the limits of action that they define for themselves. The process also highlights those areas where there may be more manoeuvrability.

The questioning about the ideology also should contain questions concerning the view the client has of other people's ideology.

- How do you think person X explains the situation?

To Mrs Dean – 'Why do you think your mother-in-law suggested that you seek a referral?' To Mr Hooper – 'What do you think your personnel officer is expecting from your coming along?' The answers to these questions essentially reveal important factors in the nature of the relationships between the client and the other person. Mr Hooper, for example, replied in answer to the question above that he thought the personnel officer was only 'really interested' in getting the work situation right because 'people were on his back'. The client's ideology of other's view essentially works in the reverse order along the ideology/potential solution sequence. It is as if the client says, 'Person A suggests a solution to me. This must mean that they think such and such about the problem.' The consultant therefore helps the client to clarify how he views the others around himself by inviting him to make the link between what people say and what view of the problem lies behind what they say. This is particularly important later when we discuss the client–consultant relationship because in this the consultant is also an 'other' and the client will have views about this 'other' as he will everyone else.

When it is clear that the relationship between the client and another person has negative elements then one can expect that the client's view of the other person's solutions to the problem will also be negative. Such a sequence in the case of Mr Hooper and his view of the personnel officer could be characterized as:

Action that resulted in event (problems in the work-group)	Not been sensible about extra-marital relationship
⇓	
Action to prevent event	Sort out marital situation
⇓	
Action as a potential solution	Give up relationship with Ms King
⇓	
Action to ensure one occurrence of solution	See counsellor

We can see here the reason why at the outset of the interview the consultant tells the client everything that is known. The client has to feel that the consultant is not taking any position with regard to how the situation has developed. The client also needs to feel it is appropriate to offer his/her own views about how others wish to see the situation dealt with. Not to reveal all that is known leaves the consultant open to the danger of being caught in a triangulated position between the client and the other person. Mr Hooper could believe that the consultant has already agreed with the personnel officer that the matter will be resolved by Mr Hooper talking about his marital situation and such a thought would result in Mr Hooper limiting the amount of flexibility that could possibly be available to the consultation process.

Continuing with the example of Mr Hooper, it was also identified that he felt he needed to do something about his relationship with Ms King and how this was creating some difficulties at work. The ideology/potential solution sequence may begin firstly with a question. 'How do you think you chose a girlfriend from the same place you work?' and to this the answer may be 'well she is very nice but I suppose it was that she was somebody that was just there.' This answer would appear to curtail the ideology/solution sequence in that it would again seem reasonable to assume that what is done is done and nothing can change. However, it is with such 'reasonable' themes that the therapist can in a humorous way introduce extreme solutions which would logically follow on within the sequence that is being constructed. In this case, for example, the extreme solution would be to find a girlfriend in another office. So the sequence would be

A.R.E. Action that resulted in event (problems in the work-group)	Begin relationship with Ms King as she is 'available' for a relationship in work place
⇓	

A.P.E. Action to prevent event	Not be in relationship with Ms King
$\Downarrow$	
A.P.S. Action as a potential solution	Leave relationship with Ms King
$\Downarrow$	
A.E.S. Action to ensure one occurrence of solution	Find another 'less local' person for relationship

The consultant introduces this extreme solution in a humorous form and perhaps in a way that would appear removed from this sequence. 'I suppose when you think about it – you wouldn't be with me today if you had begun a relationship with someone from another office – Any chance of that?' (laughs) Humour is a very useful medium for introducing difficult themes but themes which nevertheless allow the client to reflect on their position in a different way. Here, for example, the theme being introduced is that Mr Hooper has a choice about whether or not he is in a relationship and with whom he chooses to be in a relationship. The comment also validates the client's view that his problem is essentially work-based as there is no judgement made about whether he should have a girlfriend or not but merely a humorous acknowledgement that choosing to have a girlfriend in this location creates some difficulties for him.

The consultant obviously needs to be cautious with this approach as often extreme solutions are ones that have a powerful presence. With Mr and Mrs Dean we have seen that Mr Dean has the ideology of the problem related to his wife going out to work whilst Mrs Dean's is related to Mr Dean doing too little. An extreme solution following Mr Dean's ideology/solution sequence would be, 'You could stop your wife going out to work.' It would be very risky to say this humorously as it is a serious solution that they are aware of and no doubt in some way have considered. In this case there should however be an acknowledgement that Mrs Dean not going to work is a potential solution that has been rejected. Being humorous about issues concerning gender-based themes is often not helpful to the situation especially when it is reinforcing of inappropriate power balances. When such comments query the power balance they can be very useful, for example saying to Mrs Dean in a humorous way, 'Have you thought of divorcing your husband?' may have them momentarily reflect on the choices open to Mrs Dean and the potential seriousness of the situation. The consultant does need to be cautious throughout about what is said with humour and what needs to be raised in a serious and respectful manner.

Following on with Mr Hooper, it would seem important that the focus of the ideology discussion should be on his perception of how others view it.

Using the notation system we have adopted here, the following were the replies.

'Given that the problem is primarily a work one, what do you think your colleagues think about this?'

A.R.E.

I think they think that I am making it difficult for them – part of that is because Ms King doesn't get on well with some of the others. I think some of them will be thinking Ms King started it all and I've allowed it to happen. . . . Yes I think they've lost some respect for me

⇓

A.P.E.

They would think I should have been stronger and not allowed the relationship to develop

⇓

A.P.S.

If I stopped the relationship that would be the easiest for them – it would mean that I would have to sort out the relationships in the work group

⇓

A.E.S.

I should stop seeing Ms King

'So what do you think Ms King thinks of all this?'

A.R.E.

She just thinks it's fate that we got together. That the time was right for both of us. I think there is a bit of her glad she can display our relationship to other people in the group

⇓

A.P.E.

She thinks I should do something about the others in the group – get rid of them or do something like that. She sees our relationship lasting for a long time so she thinks this problem needs to be sorted out that way

⇓

A.P.S.	I should be firmer with other people and stand up to them
⇓	
A.E.S.	I need to confront people in the work group and tell the personnel manager how I am dealing with it and that I don't need his kind of help

'If your wife knew about this situation, what do you think she would think about it?'

A.R.E.	That I haven't been fair in our marriage
⇓	
A.P.E.	That I should have done more things at home
⇓	
A.P.S.	I should stop seeing Ms King
⇓	
A.E.S.	I should be firm about not seeing Ms King and give our marriage more attention

At this point the consultant could offer a general reflection based on these views. 'So it seems to you that quite a number of people believe it better for you but also for themselves that you stop the relationship with Ms King and she obviously thinks differently?' As we are dealing with the interactive elements of the ideology, an appropriate question would then be:

● 'What is your response to what you think others want you to do?'

In this question there is an invitation to the client to examine aspects of his emotional reaction to the interactive system in which he finds himself. Feelings are usually the key to meanings and at every juncture it is important to check out the client's emotional element on the reported thoughts and explanations that are being discussed. Mr Hooper's reply was 'Well I just get angry and then confused by it all – something does need to be sorted out – I know that – but the more people imply what I should do the more stubborn – or stuck I become'.

At some point in many consultation interviews a point of stuckness emerges. This is a point when the client is able to report on an aspect of feeling which indicates that he/she feels unable to do anything about a situation that would be better not existing. This is the point when the client has to confront the problem at an experiential level, when a sense of haziness emerges. At these points the consultant makes active use of the family-life cycle model and attempts to have the client consider his/her position within some general framework (see The Developmental Perspective, p. 128).

- I guess this situation can occur for men (women; families; couples) in your position in life generally – how do you think the majority of them will be dealing with it?

From being a helpless individual the question immediately places Mr Hooper in a group – and a group of people where there will be a range of responses to the situation. Mr Hooper's reply introduces an important construct that applies to himself. 'I suppose some would have the courage to throw it all up and run away with their girlfriend – others may face up to what they have to at home and sort that out.' A consultant reflection would be 'That sounds as if either way you feel you are not being coura- geous enough to make a decision and get on with the consequences of that decision?' The life-cycle question allows the client to get behind the 'this is what I should do' barrier as it places the problem within a 'normal' context and identifies the communal experience that everyone in this position can feel. It may also allow clients to explore the way in which they feel themselves to be different to other people – Mr Hooper could have replied to the question, 'There is nobody else like me because no- body else has got the horrible home life I have.' The consultant can deal with this with a straightforward ideology question. 'How do you explain that you are the only person with such a horrible home life?' The ques- tioning continually invites the client to consider the responsibility they have for what is happening to themselves. The particular sensitivities of Mr Hooper and this interview make such a question not applicable – though in other circumstances it may be. Questioning in this way results in the consultant being able only to make comments to the client about himself as the end point of any inquiry about a situation leads to identify- ing an action that is defined solely by the client. To put it another way, the consultant is only able to deal with the situation as presented by the client, and the extent to which the client takes responsibility for some of his actions within this situation then forms the limits to which the con- sultation relationship can work.

It would be at this point that the consultant in this particular interview would move on to the ideology the client has about the consultation.

However, we need to pause and consider what the general feedback would be at this time for the clients we are dealing with in this chapter.

For Mr Hooper a summary of his ideology would be:

You believe that this position arose generally because somehow you and your wife have not been giving each other enough attention. Work itself was also difficult. As Ms King was in many respects available as were you, the relationship began. It has caused problems at work as we have discussed. Your work colleagues believe that you should stop the relationship because of the difficulties that not only exist in working but also in terms of the relationship between people. You see Ms King wanting to continue with things as they are and she wants you to take some firm action to solve the problem in work. Your personnel officer seems to believe that you should sort out things on the marital front and if your wife knew, you suspect she would agree with that. Because of these pressures you have been feeling stubborn and stuck. At the bottom of it you believe it would help if you could do something 'courageous'.

Again in the situation of having a number of family members present it will be important to ask each in turn how they view these situations. In these circumstances there is an interesting dynamic, which is an advantageous feature of interviewing a number of family members at the same time and that is when the consultant is talking and questioning one person, the other family members are observers. Hence the responses of other family members are seen and heard and this has an effect itself. The important aspect of this is that each family member will contrast their own answer to every question with the answer provided by other family members; they are thus confronted with the difference between their private response and the public response of the other person. When the consultant deals with each person's account in an accepting, non-attached manner, the awareness of difference becomes not just between the private and public but also between public and public, i.e. family members confront directly the differences of opinions that they have. When clients in families are dealing with views in a public-to-public manner they may acquire all the information that is available to them to address the problematic task that is before them.

Thus it can be seen that there is a clear difference between the consulting with individuals and consulting family members with regard to the investigation of the ideology. With an individual there is more focus on how that individual views and explains the actions of others, as this places the client in an interactive system. When interviewing families the clients are present in the primary interactive system and therefore there is more focus on what individuals feel and think and how other family members respond to that information.

Turning to the situation between Mr and Mrs Dean, we have seen that they have a clear difference of opinion about the origin of the problem and hence the action that should be taken to stop the problem. Within this situation it would be important to ask about

- how the couple view Mrs Zeta Dean's contribution;
- how the couple view themselves as typical of their life-cycle stage.

The first question would be to Mrs Dean: 'How do you think your mother-in-law looks on this situation?'

A.R.E.	She thinks Mr Dean does not help me enough – I think that Jamie is difficult with her too
	⇓
A.P.E.	Mr Dean should be firmer with Jamie – by being more involved. If Jamie behaved it would make him easier to deal with
	⇓
A.P.S.	Getting Jamie sorted out – Mr Dean could do more
	⇓
A.E.S.	She thinks I've got to make sure we do the right thing for Jamie and I suppose she wants me to see if I can get Mr Dean to become more involved

Mrs Dean's response to her own ideology about her mother-in-law is that she feels her mother-in-law doesn't appreciate how much she herself feels stuck with the problem and doesn't know what to do.

The question to Mr Dean would be: 'How do you think your mother looks on the situation?'

| A.R.E. | I think she has started to interfere more. She has more time on her hands now. She thinks that we are not very capable and need help – so that will give her something to do |
| | ⇓ |

A.P.E.   If she saw us as more capable then
                                perhaps she would not interfere so
                                much

                    ⇓

A.P.S   Because she sees us as needing
                                help – she sent us to the doctor –
                                she's not giving us a chance to
                                work it out.

                    ⇓

A.E.S.   I think she needs to have Jamie
                                seen as very difficult then she can
                                help us and we will be more
                                involved with her

Mr Dean's ideology about his mother implied that he thought his wife was more able than his mother thought and this prompted another question to him concerning this relationship: 'How do you explain how your wife is dealing with your mother about this?'

'My wife is more able than she or my mother give her credit for. My wife has got so used to accepting what my mother says that she doesn't think about herself at all. Even though she may disagree sometimes, she just accepts it. There is nothing wrong with Jamie that we can't sort out – my mother may have a problem – but we can deal with him for ourselves if we are given a chance.' From Mr Dean's explanation of the situation it can be seen that the following actions may arise in terms of their dealing with the problem:

A.P.S.   Mrs Zeta Dean not to be allowed
                                to interfere so much

                    ⇓

A.E.S.   Sort out Jamie's problems between
                                ourselves as parents

Mr Dean's view of this now introduces another element into the problem which the consultant needs to follow up in terms of finding out what Mrs Dean thinks.

The question to be posed to both now remains:

- Given the situation you are in how do you think most people would deal with it?

In reply to this the differences between the couple are again revealed for Mrs Dean believes that most people would ask the other for help and Mr

Dean believes that most people would try to sort it out for themselves. Given this situation the consultant can find a way to link the two views, particularly as Mr Dean potentially could be a person who could be asked for help by Mrs Dean. Under these circumstances a 'What if' question is useful. This is a question which places time in the future and asks the individual to say what they think may be a reasonable response to an imagined scenario.

To Mrs Dean: 'As you feel it is useful to ask for help, what would happen if you asked your husband for that help?'

Here again there is an embedded suggestion within the question but it is not put in a way which suggests that this solution is any more than a potentiality. This question is also important for in the interaction around the problem events Mr Dean asks if he can help with Jamie and his wife declines the offer.

'Well I would have him help me but I am afraid that if he helps his mother will take over even more than she does. She would tell my husband off, he would become angry and all that would cause more problems.' Hence Mrs Dean has a reason why she does not adopt a particular solution because she believes that it would result in actions from others that would cause herself a bigger problem. There is a sense therefore in which Mrs Dean is dealing with the current problem so that she does not have to cope with a more problematic one. In some way Mrs Dean has a hierarchical order for the problems she faces and, like everyone else, she would prefer dealing with one at the bottom as opposed to one at the top.

There is one further element of meaning that can be investigated which again aids in the construction of a general appreciation of a problem. This involves the notion of 'catastrophic expectation' which has its origins in gestalt therapy (Perls *et al.*, 1973). This involves the element of our personal theory that predicts the worst-case scenario, the situation continuing until it is at catastrophe level. Individuals vary considerably in the extent to which they see the catastrophe as being inevitable and the closeness of the catastrophe to the present moment. A question about the catastrophic expectation serves to bring into relief those things which clients perceive as being beyond their control and those things which they may be able to influence. To put this question therefore queries whether there may be some situations in which the outcome is within our own hands.

• What is the worst thing that could happen if this problem is not solved?

Mrs Dean: 'That Jamie will become worse and worse and end up as a delinquent.'

Mr Dean: 'Well, nothing much. We'll just keep going in this way – not very happy and not sorting anything out.'

We are now in a position to offer a summary of Mr and Mrs Dean's ideology which, as with the other client, should be fed back. With Mr and Mrs Dean the consultant would need to decide whether he offers this feedback in terms of giving it on each person's ideology in turn by talking to them directly or whether to give the feedback as an interrelated whole addressed to both. This carries certain implications as the former tends to stress the conflict between family members more than the latter. The former may therefore be appropriate when the work has a marital focus with the latter being more useful in situations when there are parenting difficulties.

Mr Dean's view of the problem is that it was caused by his wife going out to work and hence Jamie began to miss his mother. His wife did not alter her expectations of how things should be done and as they needed his mother to help with child-care she has interfered more. Mrs Dean is an able woman but Mr Dean believes she has doubted this because his mother has been critical saying that they need outside help. He sees Mrs Zeta Dean as having the main problem with Jamie. Mr Dean believes many of their difficulties could be dealt with if his wife learnt to let things go and not be so fussy about housework. Mr Dean believes they can sort out their problem themselves if they are left to it and he feels this would be a much better way of doing things.

Mrs Dean's view of the problem is that her husband did not alter his expectations of family life when she began work again. She had to go back to work as they were short of money so there was no choice about that. She would like her husband to be more involved but it never seems to happen. She needs her mother-in-law's help with child-care but she does think that Mrs Dean senior has a problem with the boy. She is not sure what to do when her mother-in-law criticizes. She is afraid of the effects of this on Jamie and that his behaviour will deteriorate until he becomes a juvenile delinquent. She does think that they as a family need some help.

Having established the clients' ideology about the difficulties they face we now need to investigate the role the consultant has within this ideology and this is done in the next chapter.

4

THE CLIENT'S IDEOLOGY ABOUT CONSULTATION AND THE CONSULTANT

We now come to a pivotal point of the interview, when the consultant explores with the clients their ideology about the consultation and their relationship with the consultant. By this stage of the interview the client will have experienced the consultant as

- being clear about all that has been communicated prior to their meeting;
- accepting the client's definition of the problem;
- focusing and expanding on what actually constitutes the problem and the behaviour which defines it;
- focusing and clarifying on the thoughts and beliefs the client has about the problem;
- implying a sense that the problem is a part of a developmental process;
- implying a sense that individuals can take responsibility for their actions;
- providing regular and clarifying feedbacks on the client's statements such that a shared understanding is achieved;
- offering feedback in a manner which creates a temporally sequenced 'story' in which the consultation forms the latest part.

The consultant's attitude and orientation has therefore been consistently client-centred. At this point in the interview the consultant wishes to deal with the possibilities of the consultation in terms of the thoughts and expectations that the client had entertained on entering the consultation and these will be linked to the problem as initially outlined by the client.

The general question is therefore

- What had you hoped and expected from me today?

Clients differ in their response to this question and in very broad terms it is possible to consider some responses in terms of the stages of change model. It is also possible to categorize these responses in practical terms. Some clients wish to have an opinion given to them. Some expect and hope that they will be given advice and guidance. Some clients believe that the consultant will take some form of action on their behalf. Other clients want to be provided with an explanation of why the problem is occurring and an expectation that they will then take their own action to alleviate the problem. Some clients meet the consultant hoping that they will be offered counselling/therapy. Of course some clients arrive in the consulting office being very reluctant about attendance as they do not imagine the process as being helpful. We will deal with each of these client groups in turn.

ADVICE SEEKERS

When the general question of client expectation was asked of Mr and Mrs Dean they replied that they wanted to have some advice about how to handle their son, Jamie.

Mrs Dean: I suppose I was hoping you would give us some ideas on how we could deal with Jamie.

Mr Dean: I suppose I was expecting the same thing – you say how we should handle the boy.

Before we discuss the 'advice', it should be noted that Mr and Mrs Dean have differing attitudes to advice in that Mrs Dean is 'hoping' for this help and Mr Dean is 'expecting'. Hoping usually involves a more positive view of advice than expecting. With any issue in which two people from the same family have a different view of a particular event, the consultant will need to explore each individual's ideas so that the similarities and differences emerge. The general questions that are required are:

• What advice did you imagine I would give?

This question then needs to be followed up with

• How did you think things would be better if I offered this advice?

Again the aim of the questioning is to allow the client to explore the alternatives as they appear to themselves and the likelihood of these alternatives being successful.

- What do you think (person A) would think if I offered that advice?

As we have seen, individuals can wish to use the consultation process as a means of validating and supporting their own position in their context. The consultant wishes to assist the client in achieving a view of their position from the perspective of other parts of the system. By tracking possible responses to advice, it therefore becomes possible for the clients to verbalize that they are aware that particular forms of advice merely serve to maintain the status quo rather than act as a catalyst for change. For example, let us imagine that Mrs Dean wishes the consultant to say that his 'advice' is that her husband should do more around the house, then the next question would be 'What would your husband think if I said that?' The reply that he wouldn't listen then begins to point to the lack of value of that piece of advice. Even though it is seemingly not helpful, it does allow the consultant to identify for the other family members present what Mrs Dean would like to happen and how she feels stuck because this is not happening.

With clients who are looking for advice, it may be necessary to ask a number of questions about what non-attending family members would see as helpful advice. In this fashion, the consultant assists the client in identifying all the possible solutions that are present in the family.

- What advice do you think is likely to work?

Advice seekers appear to have one of two possible attitudes to professional advice. There are those who genuinely believe that the professional position of the consultant is such that they do have knowledge that comes from experience about how such matters can be dealt with. The clients readily acknowledge that they perceive the consultant as having some ideas about a situation in which they themselves are unsure. Typically these clients require some form of reassurance that their own natural view is a valid and important one. Other clients wish to have advice in order to maintain some position they have within their family system. This can be established by:

- If I offered you (a.b.c.) advice, how would you tell person A how it should be put into practice?

The above questions assist the consultant in determining the extent of conflict about advice in the family system. Clearly if there is the potential for a great deal of conflict then 'advice' cannot be offered – in these circumstances it will be necessary for the consultant to make it clear that there are contesting views and that it is not possible to put any advice into operation until such views find some reconciliation.

- What needs to happen for you to agree about some advice that could work?

Should a question of this nature not yield much information then the consultant from his experience could provide a list of advice that could possibly be given and then ask 'What if . . .' questions. It is not unusual for a family in a great deal of conflict to agree they would accept a particular form of advice arrived at by the consultant working through a lot of 'What if I offered you this advice?' questions.

In dealing with our example Mr and Mrs Dean, the consultant in considering their requests for 'advice' was aware of Mrs Dean saying earlier in the interview, 'I think I'm a bit lax with Jamie'. The consultant can construct some possible ideology/potential solution sequences including the advice as one of the steps. The consultant's reply would be 'I remember that you said you were lax with Jamie. I wonder if that means that the advice you need is to be firm with him?'

In essence, this 'approach' takes the clients account of their own behaviour as an action that resulted in an event (ARE) and the consultant makes a 'logical' step to 'what-if' advice with it being a likely action to prevent the event (APE). This advice therefore then becomes action as a potential solution (APS). Should Mrs Dean in this case agree that being firm would be the advice she was expecting, then the consultant could follow-up with:

- What do you think would be a practical example of that kind of advice in action?

This question is an invitation by the consultant to have the client construct an action that would ensure an occurrence of the solution. By inserting Mrs Dean's reply the sequence becomes:

ARE	Being lax with Jamie
	⇓
APE and APS	Being firm with Jamie
	⇓
AES	Telling him 'No' and sticking to it

By making the appropriate links and asking questions at the right time, we see how clients can arrive at their own 'advice'.

As the consultant is aware of the possible practical elements that this might involve with a five-year-old boy, he can then ask, 'Do you think a naughty chair might be the answer?'; 'How do you think a star chart would work?' In the family/couple context, the consultant would need to check out the effect of this advice on the other people present.

- If I gave that advice to your wife and she followed it in the way she indicated, what effect would it have on you?

Mr Dean may well reply that this would be good advice because it would stop the shouting. It would also be advice that he could follow. This naturally leads into questions about what each family member can do to help other family members follow some possible solution.

- What do you think you could do to help your wife/husband follow the advice?
- What do you think your husband/wife could do to help you follow the advice?
- What can you do to help your wife/husband help you with this advice?

These latter questions point the family/couple directly to the interactive nature of making a change in behaviour. To Mr Dean the question is about what can be done that would assist his wife in helping him to make this situation better. To Mrs Dean it is what can she do that would assist her husband in helping her make the situation better. These are important questions as they allow the consultant and the couple to address the clear gender relationship issues in a neutral way without the ascription of blame. It is appropriate that the couple find a system for sharing the chores and in this sense one of Mrs Dean's central concerns of having her husband more involved has to be confronted. The question of how she can help her husband be more involved does not imply any rightness or wrongness in the matter but merely that new behaviour needs to be encouraged and reinforced by all. Similarly the idea of helping to assist the other also implies a sharing of power and control in the situation and hence provides a useful contextual way of dealing with these issues.

As this consultation is going well, it would be a mistake to believe that once one set of 'advice' has been discussed that this in itself is sufficient. In all the discussion two other issues have been raised, namely Mrs Dean wishing to have her husband more involved and Mr and Mrs Dean being unsure of how to deal with Mr Dean's mother, Mrs Zeta Dean. Although the question of involvement is seemingly referred to in providing Jamie with a firmer approach, it would not be helpful for the consultant to assume that one issue will cover the other. A general question could then be put:

- We seem to have touched on some other issues. Were you expecting that we would look at these in terms of advice?

For some clients after the problem-solving experience of searching for the first element of advice is all they require and they will not wish to go into the process further. Should this occur the consultant should check out that in the couple/family context all the members agree with this strategy. Other clients will feel that they would wish for further advice and indicate this is so. In these cases the questioning of the consultant will follow the sequence of:

- What advice were you expecting?
- What is a practical example of this advice in action?
- What would happen if you followed that advice? (To each in turn)
- How could you help the other person to follow the advice?

Not infrequently someone will suggest some practical advice that is not acceptable to some other person. Mrs Dean might say that her husband could come home from work earlier but this might not be a solution for Mr Dean as there would be a drop in wages and he might eventually lose his job. The consultant would need to point out to the clients that if he suggested this (Mr Dean to come home early), it would not work because Mr Dean could not agree with it. Here as some advice is not destined to work, the consultant is ensuring that he is taking the responsibility for offering it. 'If I gave you that advice . . .' but that the clients individually or collectively have to take responsibility for its not being useful. 'Mr Dean would find that he could not agree . . .' The aim in these instances is to side-step any potential conflict between the consultant and client by pointing out where the responsibility for taking or not taking action clearly lies. Mrs Dean's suggestion that her husband came home early can be viewed systemically as an attempt in the context of the consultation room to have the consultant agree with her and hence form an alliance against her husband. The consultant's actions in identifying the 'advice' and reasons why it would not work is a demonstration of his being helpful to Mrs Dean. 'If I gave that advice . . .' (it is possible for me to do such things). At the same time he is helpful to other family members in that he indicates that the acceptance of the advice founders because of the interactions between the clients. Any sought-after alliance does not come to fruition as the consultant continually places back with the clients the limitations that their individual ideologies place on their collective action.

In this example Mr Dean certainly wishes to be offered advice about being more 'involved'. He suggests that if it were clearer what his wife expected of him he would have an idea of what he could do. The suggestion emerged that they should plan a week's menu together so that they were prepared each day and that they would adopt a routine at the times they arrived home so that each knew what to expect the other to do. When the consultant raised again the issue of dealing with Mrs Zeta Dean, Mrs Dean thought that if they were 'getting their act together themselves' they would naturally deal with her mother-in-law in a better way. Mr Dean agreed with this.

We can now summarize the Deans' ideology of consultation. In slightly different ways they both had the expectation that they would be offered some advice. Mrs Dean was more keen for this initially but as the session progressed Mr Dean increasingly saw an advantage in their being offered help in this way. As they agreed there was a need to be firmer with Jamie, following an embedded suggestion from the consultant a practical task to address this issue emerges which the couple find acceptable. The consultant, being mindful that the difficulty with the little boy was the presenting problem, checks out their ideology of consultation for the other issues that have emerged. The couple were agreed that they would welcome some suggestions on how approaching their household chores another way would be helpful. They both thought that planning a routine together would be a suggestion they would be happy with. Mr Dean in particular believed that if they tackled these problems successfully then the difficulties they were experiencing with his mother would diminish.

In some family/couple contexts it is not unusual for there to be agreement that advice (or opinion or an explanation) is being sought but regardless of the best effort of the consultant it is not possible to find advice (opinion or explanation) that the couple can agree upon. In these cases the consultant will move toward making the general comment, 'You seem not to be able to agree on any possible line of action. My advice is that I am unable to give you advice.' As a lead in to this position the consultant would ask:

- What would you say if I said it was not possible to offer any advice about your difficulty as I am unable to find any common ground on which to base such advice?

In marital situations particularly where the couple have completely opposed views as to what should occur, the consultant will need to confirm the stuckness of their entrenched positions. This is often necessary before there can be some movement in the readiness to change the cycle of interaction. The way in which the consultant deals with these types of clients is discussed in Chapter 5.

OPINION SEEKERS

In his reply to the query about his expectation about consultation Mr Hooper is quite clear. 'Well I think I would be grateful for your opinion about the situation I am in – you know, say what you really think?' Mr Hooper's reply places him with the group of people who wish the consultant to offer his personal/professional view so that they can take it away and do with it what they wish. With opinion seekers there are then three supplementary questions.

● What would you like me not to say?

Opinion seekers do not have a view of the consultant's opinion as being a blank sheet. Well before the consultation they have a view of the possible things that could be said with a special emphasis on the things they would really dislike. The opinion therefore has 'limits'. It would not be helpful to offer the client 'opinions' which he would reject, for clearly opinions from an 'outside' other need to fall within those positive and acceptable possibilities that the client holds. The consultant therefore ensures that he is familiar with the limits that the client's ideology has created.

Mr Hooper: 'Well I wouldn't like you to say that you agree with the personnel manager and that I should sort out my marriage for the sake of the firm. To be honest I expected you to say that – you know because they are paying and all that.'

● If I do give you my opinion, who will you tell – what will you do with it?

Very often opinion seekers wish for an opinion of a certain nature so that they can have the consultant 'on their side' when they talk to someone else. In itself this is neither a good nor a bad thing for the consultant needs to evaluate the nature of the relationship between the client and the other person before determining his exact response. The evaluation obviously is carried out with the client and it must be within the context of the presenting problem. So should Mr Hooper say he wishes for an opinion that will help him just to get the personnel officer off his back; the consultant would need to explore how a particular opinion might allow this to happen so that the work situation seems less problematic. His actual reply was: 'I think I need to sort some things out with Ms King and it would be helpful if I had a perspective from another angle to think about it.'

The implication of this is clear for it does indicate some change in the most important ideology/solution sequence in that a solution to the difficulty is beginning to be seen in having a conversation with Ms King about whether or not things need to be different.

- What would you like me to say?

Mr Hooper: 'Before we discussed this I think what I really wanted was for you to tell me that you thought I was doing the very best thing I could – that you agreed with me. I suppose now having talked about it I would like you to say that all this can be sorted out – you know, that if things are approached one after another then it won't be such a problem.'

Mr Hooper demonstrates that he had some preconceived ideas about how the consultant would behave and these have developed during the course of the consultation process. Mr Hooper started by looking for a partisan view and has moved to a position where he appears to be asking for reassurance that there will be a satisfactory outcome if he struggles with the problem.

Should the client, unlike Mr Hooper, provide an answer to this question that indicates ambivalence about different opinions, then the consultant may usefully explore the varieties of options with 'What if I said . . .' questions. These are questions where the consultant goes through the possible alternative 'opinions' as if he owned them but allowing the 'as if' to imply a distance and a 'let's pretend' quality. In Mr Hooper's case one might have asked 'What if I said I agreed with the personnel officer?' 'What if I told you I thought you were on the right lines?', etc. These questions allow the client to deal with the reality of these views in an interactive setting rather than just as something that is going on inside his head. As the consultant wishes for his own 'view' to be based on a thorough understanding of the client's perspective, the 'let's pretend' aspect of these questions permits the exploration of themes introduced by the client without their becoming attached to the person of the consultant. 'What if I . . .' questions have a great utility and impact throughout the consultation process.

In providing a brief summary of Mr Hooper's ideology of consultation we can see that he has through the process of the interview altered his perspective. Mr Hooper is now asking for someone else's opinion on his situation but it is not just anyone's opinion, it is that of the consultant. As the session has progressed the consultant has become a 'significant other' for Mr Hooper at least for a short period. The personal contact of the interview has resulted in Mr Hooper wanting to know what the consultant thinks. He now believes that he has to sort out some issues with Ms King and he is asking for reassurance that a solution can be found.

ACTION EXPECTORS

The category of client that can be termed action expectors are those clients who attend with the expectation that the consultant will take some action on their behalf involving a third party. For instance in our examples, Mr and Mrs Dean could have expected the consultant to discuss Jamie with the school and Mr Hooper could have expected the consultant to have a particular type of discussion with the personnel manager or another person in authority. Common 'third parties' include schools and education authorities (for children's problems), residential homes (for problems with the elderly), housing departments (for all sorts of problems) and line managers (for work-related problems). The most typical action being hoped for is that the consultant will persuade some institution or person to do something different as this will resolve the difficulty for the client. The questions to ask such clients are:

- What exactly did you want me to say to them?
- What effect do you think that would have?
- What would happen if they don't do that?
- Is there anything else that can be done to get what it is you want?
- Is there anyone else that can help you in this way?
- What disadvantages do you see in my doing what you ask?

The aim of the consultant is to fully explore the link the client has made between the presenting problem and the expected action of the consultant. Such links could include:

- The child will not be so upset if you tell my solicitor to stop my ex-husband seeing the child.
- The child would be easier to control if we lived in a house rather than a flat. Please tell the housing department.
- I will be better able to deal with my difficulty if you tell the personnel manager that my line manager is hassling me.
- If you spoke to the doctor he would arrange for my mother to have a place in a residential home and that would stop the family's problems.

THEORY SEEKERS

Many clients come with the awareness that there is some problem for themselves and feel rather perplexed or frustrated that they do not understand how this problem came into being and how it manages to continue. Theory seekers are individuals and families who exemplify the point that people seek to make sense of their world and if their usual way of understanding does not seem to apply then they feel stuck and rather uncomfortable. With these types of client a general reflection in the form of a question would be:

- So, if I find a way of helping you explain this difficulty to yourself (yourselves) then you would feel you were getting somewhere?

The question that then follows is:

- When you try to explain this to yourself, what ideas do you come up with?

This question is an invitation to have the client(s) explore how they think about the problem and how those thoughts do not seem to provide a satisfactory explanation to themselves. In many respects this is a repetition of those questions that were asked earlier in the interview. Now, however, they are being asked when the client's expectations are under discussion, which creates a slightly different context to the initial enquiry. Theory seekers tend to benefit from this latter form enquiry as in the initial phase of the interview they seldom perceive their responses to the explanation questions as containing ideas for which they can take responsibility. To ask these questions in a different frame therefore offers the task to the clients of reflecting on and following through with the implications of their 'theory'.

> Ms Andrews was a 28-year-old woman who was single and living alone. Her parents both became ill and in order to help them it was necessary for her to move into her parents' home. The demands of their illnesses and of her job were considerable. Ms Andrews sought help from a counsellor, not so much because of the demands placed on her but more because she was feeling very resentful toward her parents and these feelings resulted in her feeling guilty and angry with herself. When she saw the counsellor for consultation she said she wanted to find out the reason for her strong feelings of resentment. The counsellor established that Ms Andrews believed that good daughters should not have negative feelings about caring for their parents. The counsellor asked questions such as:
>
> - Do you know any good daughters? What do they say to you?

This introduced the maternal aunt's comments about her daughter, i.e. Ms Andrews' cousin. From this point the discussion moved on to how some family members help and some hinder.

- Do you believe that good daughters always do the dutiful thing?

This led on to a conversation about the nature of positive and negative emotions for adults.

- If you could deal with this situation without having to worry about your thoughts and feelings, what might you be doing different practically?

Ms Andrews in response to this question felt that she would not be behaving in any significantly different way.

The example demonstrates how the consultant constructs questions from the client's frame of reference. The 'theory' element then is seen as just another component in the client's ideology in response to their psychosocial situation. The consultant then has the role of holding onto the gestalt of the client's perspectives so that when the time comes to offer feedback, the client is presented with his/her overall framework rather than just one element of it.

General theory seekers of the kind 'we want to know why' permit the consultant to discuss with them the nature of their views about all aspects of the situation. A consultation interview will then follow a path similar to action expectors and advice seekers. There are, however, some particular categories of theory seekers that need mention.

1. The person who expects the consultant to offer a particular theory which he/she can then reject.

> Mr Parsons sought help from a consultant as his wife was having an affair. He stated that he wanted help to understand why. He told the consultant 'I know you will say that she is doing this because she loves him more than me – but I know that is not true.' The consultant's questions were
>
> - What if I offered you reason X?
>
> Mr Parsons: 'No it's not that.'
>
> - What if I said there was no reason?
>
> Mr Parsons: 'There must be.'
>
> For Mr Parsons the consultant will be offering him the experience of examining the structure of his thoughts in which everything is leading to

the one focus, i.e. his wife does not love him, only for this to then be rejected by Mr Parsons. The consultant will need to feedback at some point, 'It seems however we approach this topic, there does not appear to be an acceptable explanation. The one you keep expecting and coming back to is that your wife does not love you any more – and that is the one that is most unacceptable to you.'

2. The person who expects to find a reason 'deep' within themselves being revealed by 'psychoanalysis', 'hypnosis' or some other arcane process in which the client believes they give up control of their mind to the consultant. These clients typically make statements such as, 'I expected you to psychoanalyse me so that you could find out why I am doing this.' For these clients the consultant wishes to explore what they are expecting will be inside and why they believe that whatever is inside is locked away.

- Why do you think it will be necessary to do something different than just talk to you?
- What do you think is at the root of it all?

Again it may be necessary for the consultant to investigate via the 'what if' questions that tap into that element of meaning which involves 'catastrophic' expectations. In the case of theory seekers the consultant asks the questions:

- What is the worst thing we could find out if we hypnotize you?
- What is the thing you most dread being the reason?

The consultant would then embark on a conversation about this with the client. It will, however, be just as important to ask the client what the 'best' case scenario would be:

- What if somebody did hypnotize you and they found out something that would really please you – what would that be?

At varying points in a consultation interview the discussion of 'best' and 'worst' outcomes provides a useful medium for allowing the client to consider the range of possibilities that is open to them. Such questions also indicate to the client that hypnosis is not something that the consultant embarks on in this manner.

3. In child-focused cases it is not unusual for parents to request that the consultant 'read the mind' of a child. Typically there is a problem behaviour which the parents assume must be due to a deep-seated

problem and they want the consultant to find out what it is. The expectation is that the consultant will take the child into some quiet room and in a manner unavailable to parents, talk to the child such that the innermost workings of their minds are revealed. The explanation for the child's behaviour, it is then believed, will then become apparent. Street *et al.* (1991) have discussed how this particular issue can be dealt with.

General questions that become relevant when clients come along seeking theories are those that explore potential solution actions that are implicated in the theory offered.

- Supposing we found an explanation for this and we agreed that it was . . . What would you think about it? What would you do differently because of this explanation?
- Supposing we considered that explanation . . . was the more likely one, what would you do differently if that was offered to you as an explanation?

As always the consultant is exploring the possible differences in behaviour between the present and the future and in particular is having the client focus on future action. This is a focus that places the responsibility for what happens next with the client.

COUNSELLING CLIENTS

Some clients expect that the consultant will talk to them in a way that allows them to explore their feelings and thoughts. A number of clients in this category will have received counselling in the past and hence have been inducted into the approach. Some clients believe that this method of dealing with their difficulty is the obvious and appropriate 'treatment'. Although it would appear that these clients are ready and available for counselling there are as many potential problems, not least the assumption that they know what other choices are available. In a manner similar to the other groups the expectations, the personal limits and the ideology/solution link need to be explored.

- What themes do you expect us to cover?
- What do you expect will happen when we talk about these things?
- How will you know when we don't have to talk about these things any more?
- Did you have any ideas about how often you wanted to meet to talk?

RELUCTANT CLIENTS

Some clients attend having a mish-mash of expectations about why they are sitting in the consultation room. Essentially their reply to 'Why have you come today?', is 'I was sent.'

- If person X had not suggested to you that you should come along then would you have bothered to come?
- Who is the person who is expecting most from this – you or the person who suggested you should come?

All reluctant clients gain an experience of the consultation process and the consultant can ask later whether or not what has happened in the interview has altered their perceptions in any way.

- Now that you have met me and we have started to talk about things, do you have a different view of coming along?

Some clients may come to the view that what is on offer could be useful to them, whilst others will maintain their reluctance. This may be related to their position in the readiness to change cycle (see Stages of Change Model, p. 139). With those who continue in their reluctance the counsellor should discuss with the clients the differences of opinion that exists between them as clients and the referrer.

- Can you help me understand how the person who referred you thought it would be a good idea while you believe otherwise?

The exploration that occurs here is an examination of whether the problem is in a sense the referrer's or the client's. The question addresses the relationship between client and referrer, a relationship in which the consultant will not intervene as the consultation is for the client. The consultant is not interested in entering into a negotiation about the referrer's intentions or actions. He is interested in establishing how this particular client views the process of consultation and how this process can be completed in the most helpful manner.

EXPECTATIONS OF THE CONSULTANT AS A PERSON

We have seen that the consultant is not only interested in forming a relationship with the client but that he is also interested and able to comment on the nature of the workings of that relationship. To assist this the consultant can ask the client to consider the expectations that they held about him as a person before they met. This gives the client permission to consider the interaction that is occurring between them as a series of events that can be commented on. It also allows for there to be some 'clearing of the decks' in the sense that in verbalizing these expectations, it allows the client and consultant to jointly discount them, thereby permitting themselves to form a relationship that is constructed in the 'here and now'. It allows the client to meet the consultant as he is and allows the client to feel more freely that the interview and 'consultation' are truly co-constructed. By permitting comments on the person of the consultant, the consultant can be a person and it is from meeting person-to-person that processes of change and healing can occur.

- What kind of person did you think I would be?
- What kind of questions did you think I would ask?
- What did you imagine I would think of you?

Once the consultant has enquired into the expectations about the consultation all the information is now at hand in order to make the consultation statement and this will be dealt with in the next chapter.

5

MAKING THE 'CONSULTATION STATEMENT'

In every social context each person has a set of ideas about how the interactions in that context will proceed, expectations concerning how others will behave in particular circumstances. Within the context of talking to a professional about a difficulty, the general expectation is that the client will outline whatever the difficulty is, the professional may seek some clarification, the professional will then respond in some way and the next step will be decided upon so that action in the future can be determined. Obviously each context will carry with it different rules and expectations but in terms of discussing a personal difficulty or worry, the general expectation is not that different from other professional/client interactions. In terms of the approach outlined in this book the consultation statement is that element of the process where the consultant makes his formal and considered response to what the client has said. It is a means of punctuating the general expectations of this professional/client context as it brings to an end one element of the process involving the client and the consultant and it begins another part which concerns the client alone. Essentially the consultant meets the general expectation of making a response within the framework of the client's ideology about the consultation and the consultant. The consultant wishes to do this in a manner which clearly indicates that this response is based totally on the view that was constructed by both of them within their preceding private conversation. A subsidiary expectation of any professional contact is that the professional in declaring a response publicly will base it on professional knowledge and expertise and that this professional response can be differentiated from what the professional may think privately. In the therapeutic consultation approach the consultant wishes to emphasize that he/she considers that there has been personal contact with the client in which the consultant has been clear about his private and professional thoughts and actions.

In essence the consultant provides an overview summary of all that has gone on in the interview to date. It is therefore a general feedback statement given as a view from the consultant himself. The difference between this and a straightforward paraphrase or reflection is that the consultant in the manner of his language clearly takes some responsibility for making these particular statements. This is achieved by the consultant prefixing some statements with 'I' and explaining how he arrived at some ideas from the conversation that has occurred. For example:

- Well we've discussed what has happened to you and your ideas about this and I have been trying to put all these things together so what we are left with is . . .
- As we've been talking I have been trying to keep the central points together and for me they seem to be . . .
- Well I guess it's now time for me to think aloud to see what sense I am making of all this so that we can work out how I can help best.

What then follows will be:

1. A résumé of the historical version of the problem, particularly identifying life-cycle themes.
2. An overview summary of the client's ideology of the problem.
3. An overview summary of the client's ideology of the consultation process.

These elements will be a recap of the feedback that has gone on before but the consultant still needs to ensure that he/she is following the client's story and ideas as they evolved in the conversation with the client about the problem. The consultant will try to continually use the language of the client and if in the process of the interview the client has redefined, relabelled or reframed any aspect, it is important that the consultant indicates awareness of those changes.

- . . . and you feel it was difficult with your wife . . . at first it seemed like irritation to you but as we talked you thought it was more anger.

As the consultant goes through the 'story' as it emerged it becomes clear to both client and consultant that if the consultant is to offer an opinion, advice, explanation etc., despite the client's ambivalences there is only one consultant response that is possible and acceptable. This is the view of future action that the client is most able to take responsibility for. The process is therefore one of validation of the client's view and an empowering of their problem-solving strategy. In essence with the consultant statement, the consultant is saying to the client, 'I've listened to all you have to say about this, heard your ideas about what you would wish to do in the future, considered how you wish to use me and I agree with you.'

TIMING AND THE CONSULTATION STATEMENT

Before we present our examples it is necessary to offer some thoughts as to the timing of making the consultation statement. Different consultants and clients will vary in the speed with which they travel through the tasks of the consultation interview. On some instances the task will be completed within one session – and for some clients it may be useful to arrange for this session to be longer than the 'therapeutic hour'. Other clients and situations will require two appointments in order to complete the tasks. Should two sessions be necessary, it is important that the interviews be scheduled relatively close together; the client requires the experience of the interview procedure to be a consistent integrated whole and time lapses of longer than two weeks between sessions do not allow for this. The client needs to be given the clear message that it is only for the sake of using time effectively that there is to be this separation. In these circumstances it is also advisable before the end of the first session to ascertain briefly the nature of the client's expectations about the process so that the client knows that in some way these expectations can and will be met.

Regardless of whether 'the' interview is one or two sessions long, the statement should be clearly placed toward the end of the process. Again for some clients the process may well be less than the therapeutic hour, the end coming when it comes rather than at a set distance from the beginning. There then are two options for how the statement will be delivered:

1. Delivering the statement right at the end of the interview. Here the consultant seeks to provide his/her input and then stop the interview process. Apart from some polite dealing with the immediate queries the aim is to prevent the client and consultant from interacting following this intervention. This may be deemed valuable if the consultant is working within a strategic framework. It may also be the method of choice where there is conflict in a family or couple and the consultant has provided a view on that conflict (see Chapter 4). It will be likely that the clients will need to address their conflict through the medium of what has been said to them in the statement and this is certainly best done away from the interview room.

2. Delivering the statement at a point where the consultant can assist the clients in reflecting on their response to it. This may be considered appropriate when clients have seemingly changed their thinking within the interview process. What is important when the statement is provided in this way is that the consultant does not rigidly hold onto it as his view. It is very possible that the consultant has misheard or misstated or misjudged in some way what has gone on before and even at this stage in the process the client may offer correction or ask for further clarification. It should be remembered that the consultant is attempting to remain broadly within the client's frame of reference and this applies just as much to the period following the making of a statement. The consultant needs to be adept at judging when clients are entering into the mode of clarifying their frame as opposed to attempting to recruit the consultant to one side of a conflict in a family. Consultants should therefore feel confident of the benefits in remaining neutral in the immediate post-delivery phase.

With increasing experience we have found that it is possible to offer a consultation statement without having to pause or create a space between the interview and the delivery phase. Individuals training in the approach benefit from taking a little reflection time between these phases in the process. Trainees may need to leave the interview room for a short while in order to 'collect their thoughts' whilst more experienced learners can readily take some time out of the interview process and ask the client to bear with them whilst they make some notes. There are no set rules for how one does this. It is in the end down to individual style.

OFFERING A CONSULTATION STATEMENT

In order to present to the reader the broader means of constructing consultation statements we shall discuss the two principal examples that we have developed. These are examples of opinion seekers and advice seekers. Following a discussion on the writing of a consultation statement as a letter we shall then provide examples of the other types of identified clients.

When providing the statement in a family/couple situation as in the case of Mr and Mrs Dean the consultant needs to use his non-verbal communication to ensure that he indicates from which person he took the main piece of information which he is relating. It is important not to look at the wrong person when providing this information as it can very easily imply an alliance is formed with one person against another. When referring to the couple in a general way then non-verbal signs should be made that all are being referred to.

Advice Seekers

'Well Mr and Mrs Dean, I suppose now that we've talked through it all, it is my turn to say what sense I have made of the difficulty you are facing. You have two children and it sounds as if you will not be planning on having any more. Like a lot of families with young children, sometimes they seem a handful, the chores seem never-ending and you need all the money you can get. Whilst the children were younger, you, Mrs Dean, remained working at home and Mr Dean continued in his job. Finances became a struggle and you decided that, if possible, Mrs Dean would find a job outside of the home. The major difficulty you saw in organizing this was in getting the children looked after, particularly after nursery and play group. As Mr Dean's mother was used to looking after the children and as she seemed to have time on her hands, you all agreed that she would pick up the children until Mrs Dean came to collect them. You all knew Jamie could be more of a problem than his sister as he does have a tendency not to do as he is told. Mrs Dean, you feel this can be dealt with well if you have enough energy to deal with him and Mr Dean, you feel he responds to you well anyway.

Things started to become more difficult at this point in your family's life with Jamie's behaviour apparently getting worse. Mrs Dean Senior was then ringing up to check on how things were and she was reporting that she was finding him difficult. It was because of the concerns that she told you about, that you, Mr Dean, sought an appointment with the family doctor which your wife attended and then you ended up seeing me.

What we then found out is that you, Mrs Dean, have tended to keep to yourself your concerns about Jamie, you have wanted your husband to help more around the house and although you are grateful for your mother-in-law's help you are anxious in case she tries to take over. As you thought about this, what you wanted was your husband to recognize the difficulty and then do something active about it.

You, Mr Dean, have not been so concerned about Jamie's behaviour but you are aware of the difficulties in the home at the end of the day. You are not sure what your wife expects of you, you feel she just gets angry with you and when this happens you just leave believing that an argument will only make matters worse. You both feel this needs to be sorted out to prevent things becoming worse in the future and to try to make things better now.

As you know, moving from being a housewife to a shop-worker *and* a housewife is a difficult change to make just as it is difficult to move from having a wife at home all the time to a situation where everyone is out at work during the day. Any and every family will need to make a lot of changes and adaptations to deal with this.

As we looked at how you managed this, it did seem as though it was difficult to get to talk about the problem in any way. The only person Mrs Dean mentions her concerns to are to her mother-in-law and she in turn has a view that Mr Dean could do more. Mr Dean, you also think that you as parents are both more capable than your mother gives you credit for. You both feel that it is best if your mother does not get too involved except just as a grandmother. This is a fairly common feeling among young couples about their in-laws.

Although you both agree, it would be good if Mrs Dean didn't have to go out to work, you also agree that there is no alternative. This makes you both feel frustrated and a little sad, but again, it does seem to be a typical problem for families at this stage in their development.

You have asked me to give you some advice about ways of dealing with domestic chores and the managing of Jamie. In our discussion you both thought that more of an organized routine including a menu for the family would be helpful. I suppose this could involve your sitting down sometime before you do the shopping on Saturday (and I'm not sure if one or the other of you or both should do that) and writing out a menu. You also know that it would help if you both had an agreement about the chores that need to be attended to at the end of the day. Then when you are both there you will have an agreed plan about who is doing the food and who is looking after the children etc. It may be useful to swap these jobs around and I don't know whether you should just let that happen or whether you should set it up beforehand. We will obviously need to see how this strategy is working at a later date.

With regard to Jamie, you both are agreed that he needs to be managed more firmly. For boys of five I take that as meaning something like; if they are asked to do something once or twice and they do not obey, something should be used as a quick and immediate 'punishment' – for example 30 seconds on a 'naughty' chair – a sort of time out. Points or stars can be given for good behaviour – which could be changed for 'special rewards'. You may decide that you need to keep a wall chart – some parents do. I would guess if you start to do this he will be more difficult for a while until he learns that some new rules apply to him. Obviously my advice would be for you both to do this and his grandmother should also apply the same rules. I am not sure how you would arrange to tell her about your new rules for the lad, that is something you will decide for yourselves. Although Mrs Dean Senior's contribution may at times not be helpful, I agree with you that as you sort out these difficulties with Jamie between yourselves this problem will probably become less of an issue.'

A particular type of advice seeker that should be mentioned are those families and/or couples who have very different views as to what should happen. With these clients the consultant in the statement should feed back each opposing view and clearly indicate that such are the differences of opinion that it is not possible for him to offer advice to them as a group. The aim in these circumstances is to provide all the clients with a consultation on the rigidity of their systems' functioning in this area; this level of comment is more likely to aid in the process of moving matters forward. In taking this line the consultant will certainly need to suggest other alternatives that they can take individually or jointly.

> Mr and Mrs Moore sought advice from a marital counsellor. Mr Moore had been receiving individual counselling for some time and had come to a conclusion that he was unhappy with his relationship with his wife. His counsellor suggested he and his wife seek help together. Mrs Moore reluctantly attended with her husband. She did not feel there to be a major problem; she could not see any prospect for change in herself but she said she would be resigned to any changes her husband made. Mr Moore wished to feel closer to his wife and wished for her to discuss matters. Mrs Moore saw little need to discuss things, either privately with her husband or 'publicly' with the marital counsellor. It was apparent that this situation had maintained itself for some while.
>
> The marital counsellor adopted a therapeutic consultation approach. At the end of their session she told them that she could not offer any advice as there was little agreement on which to base jointly appropriate advice. If she suggested the case for counselling Mr Moore would be pleased and his wife displeased. If she suggested that they did not come for counselling then vice versa. As Mrs Moore appeared content to have things remain as they were then all she could advise was that she continue in this way. As Mr Moore was clearly unhappy with the situation all she could advise him was to recommence individual counselling as it appeared to help him and obviously at some point in the future he may need to make a decision about whether to continue with his marriage or not and that would be a decision for him alone as it did not appear possible for them to mutually discuss matters at this point in their relationship.
>
> The consultant informed Mrs Moore that if she required to see someone individually she could arrange for that to happen. Some six months later Mrs Moore rang requesting some names of counsellors as her husband had decided to move away and she wished to talk through the implications of this.

Opinion Seekers

We can now turn to Mr Hooper and the difficulties he faces.

'Mr Hooper, now that I understand what the issues are about, what I would like to do is recap so that we have the background to the opinion I have formed. It might be helpful to start by putting things into the sequence of their development. Your wife and you begin not to get on and it feels to you this is because she is not attentive enough. This is at the same time that work doesn't go too well. We're not sure if these two things are linked in any way. You know you feel like doing something different, you find yourself getting on well with Ms King and you begin a relationship with her. In a sense, we now have two issues which are problems for you – your relationship and home life on the one hand and your relationship and work on the other. You would like to keep these things separate. Given the way you came to see me through the personnel officer, what you wished to address as the main problem with me is the 'work' one.

In your own mind you are not too sure why things seemed to be going wrong for you but certainly your relationship with Ms King gave you an exciting feeling and in some senses this made things feel better.

Your relationship with Ms King causes difficulties at work because of your position and in some sense what is happening is undermining your authority there. A number of your colleagues find it difficult and it would appear that Ms King's approach doesn't help matters. You have felt confused by all these things and not certain of the way forward but because so many people, such as the personnel manager, your colleagues and I suppose, if she knew, your wife, are saying you must stop the relationship it makes you stubborn and you just carry on. This is even when, for your own reasons, you wish to limit your time with Ms King but despite this you find yourself continuing in the same way. You know that Ms King has different expectations of the relationship to yourself and some of the agreements you have made about your time together have been broken by her. This all adds to your confusion about the situation.

As we have discussed, given your age, the nature of your job and all the other trappings that go along with being you, it is not unexpected that you should be unclear of the way forward for yourself. Many men find themselves thinking about the issues of marriage, family, occupation and wonder if it is the time to make a change, and it could feel as if it could be the last chance to make a change. I suppose this is why it feels as if it must be a big decision you have to make and that to make it, you must have a great deal of courage. It's a major life choice and not unsurprisingly you have been feeling that you haven't been equal to making such a big decision. I'm not sure if you would have had a discussion with somebody such as myself if the personnel officer hadn't suggested it to you. However, in the process of talking about it together I understand that you feel it would be useful hearing my reaction, having my opinion, so that you can listen to somebody with a different perspective on matters.

In my opinion you certainly are very aware that a clear decision needs to be taken and you know you have to make it. You also appear to be very aware that in order to make this decision you have to go through a process of sorting out different bits with different people. I feel you have a very good grasp of your situation and this should enable you to do this. The only thing that I'm not sure of is what you actually need to do for yourself as a person and it may be that at this moment you don't know.

That's where I have got to in all this and that is my opinion. Some people like to see what I have said written in a letter and I would be glad to do that for you.'

WRITING THE CONSULTATION STATEMENT AS A LETTER

A feature of this approach is the routine transcription of the verbally given statement into the form of a letter (see The Written Word in Therapeutic Encounters, p. 149). This is not an approach where the statement would only be offered via letter; the essential element is providing the statement verbally. The letter will therefore follow the form and language of the statement; however, because of the nature of the written word these features need to be tighter and well thought out. It is advisable therefore that if a consultation letter is to be sent, the consultant make some quick notes just prior to offering the statement and certainly immediately following the end of the interview. In order to preserve the personal and intimate essence of the statement the consultant should write the letter as soon as is possible. Our practice, however, has not been to write the letter immediately following the interview but some hours later or even the next day. We have found that this slight delay allows for some further reflection with the result that there is an improved distillation of the ideas provided to the clients. However this time is organized it is important that the client receive the letter within ten days of the interview and sooner if possible. Letters sent after this time do not appear to have the same impact as the emotional memories and active experiencing of the consultation interview will have diminished or been overlaid by other events after this time. If not received quickly other meanings will have been created and the letter only then serves to undermine the development of what is changing rather than enhance it. As the letter is likely to be shorter and less elaborated than the statement, some simple guidelines about the letter design should be followed.

1. Always mention the referral process and the problem that was being referred.
2. Outline the problem as perceived within a historical framework. This section should immediately follow the comments on the referral process.
3. Cast issues in developmental terms.
4. Views should always be syntonic with client ideology and use important phrases and terms from the actual sessions.
5. If some interactions have been identified as unhelpful, neutrally indicate these.
6. Make 'you' and 'I' statements as this signifies the personal aspect of the client–consultant relationship.
7. Even if there is clearly one favoured solution, the consultant should always indicate that there are choices on offer and that these choices are the responsibility of the client, not the consultant.

Mr and Mrs Dean's letter is produced below.

Dear Mr and Mrs Dean,

It was good to meet with you the other day. As you know, Dr Jones referred you to me as there had been some concerns about Jamie's behaviour. I understand, Mr Dean, that your mother suggested that something needed to be done about this and that you made the appointment with Dr Jones that led you on to seeing me.

It would seem that Jamie has always been a lively boy and he has always needed firm control from someone 'one step ahead of him'. In the past you dealt with this well but when you agreed that it would be financially helpful for Mrs Dean to work outside the home, it appeared to make matters worse, particularly from your point of view, Mrs Dean. It also seemed that you both had some difficulty in changing the chores and responsibilities around the home so that it made it easier for Mrs Dean to be at work. As we discussed, this is a task that most people face when they have a young family to provide for and the parents have to return to work.

You have tried to deal with this problem but what seems to happen is that you, Mrs Dean, become angry with your husband. You, Mr Dean, don't know what to do so you leave the room and in the end nothing gets sorted out. Both of you dislike this and you both are watchful of Mrs Dean Senior beginning to interfere as you do not want this to happen.

You have asked me to give you some advice on handling Jamie and managing the chores. From our discussion it would appear that Jamie would benefit from being dealt with more firmly. I think this could mean using a star-chart for good behaviour and if he is naughty using an instant, short time out, e.g. the naughty chair idea. Obviously it would help if all the adults concerned with Jamie would keep to these rules. In terms of the chores and sharing these fairly, then it seemed as if having a weekly menu would let you both know what was to be done on returning home from work. Mr Dean you said you would find following a routine easier to do.

I am not sure how you will make this advice work out in practice but I would expect there to be some false starts, mistakes and uncertainty before you get it right for yourselves.

We have agreed that we will have a follow-up meeting in six weeks time and I look forward to seeing both of you then.

Theory Seekers

As we saw in Chapter 4, the consultant clarifies with the client the theory that is most likely to gain acceptance by the client and follows this up with the question:

- If we find it is (this) explanation, what would you do differently?

The consultation statement is then built around the response to the second question rather than just focusing on the acceptable theory. The consultant will be exploring and clarifying with the client those actions that are possible and perceived by the client as being within their repertoire of behaviour. Once the consultant has an impression of this, then it becomes possible to offer a consultation statement based on the acceptable theory and the behaviours that are consequent on that theory.

With theory seekers the consultation statement should contain

- those potential explanations the client indicates as acceptable;
- the expectation the client has of what will follow once the theory has been 'discovered' or 'confirmed';
- a statement that from discussing matters with the client the consultant is able to come to a view about possible theories;
- the most useful and acceptable theory from the consultant's perspective.

An example of this is provided below.

Dear Mrs Nichols,

Thank you for coming along to see me the other day with Glyn. I am pleased that we were able to have a good discussion about the difficulties that you have with Glyn, particularly as he is a boy who has no difficulty in saying what he thinks. You told me Glyn has always been a bit difficult to manage and when you and his father were together it required a joint effort. You have found ways of dealing with him since your divorce three years ago but in the last year, since he went to the Comprehensive School, he has been mixing with an older set of boys, staying out late and sometimes skipping school. Previously when you had any sort of trouble with him you would call his father who would tell him off and sometimes, if necessary, visit your home to tell him off. Unfortunately the demands of his new family prevent Mr Nichols from continuing to do this.

You have been wondering why Glyn's behaviour appears to be getting worse. You were hoping that I would be able to find the cause of the problem as it now is. From just talking about it we did isolate three possible reasons for his behaviour:

(a) That he is upset that his Dad has a new baby and he is behaving the way he is to get his own back.

(b) That he doesn't like your new partner, Roy, and given that Roy has only been around for about six months, a part of Glyn's behaviour may be related to this.

(c) That in the past his father was the main 'boss' of him and that you have not been able as yet to be as firm a 'boss' as he needs. As a result he is taking advantage of your not being firm enough with him.

My impression is that Glyn is at that stage of life when he is moving from being your 'little' boy into being an adolescent (and one of the big boys). Clearly his move to secondary school will have emphasized this change in status to him. At this phase of development, it is not unusual to find that boys are more argumentative with their mothers. This happens whether they are in a single parent or a step family.

Having talked to you about the difficulty and having met with and talked to Glyn, my view is that Glyn is a boy who has actually been helped by both you and Mr Nichols to cope very well with your divorce. However, he is a boy who benefits and is used to authoritative parental control with there being one person who is clearly taking the major responsibility for him. Circumstances have certainly changed for him and you over the recent past and these changes may be linked to his present behaviour. However, the principal reason for his current difficult behaviour appears to me to be that he is making some use of the fact that his father's reduced availability has left a space which as you said you have not yet been able to fill.

Even though Glyn has a lot to say, he certainly does not have any ideas about the reasons for his own behaviour and I would not expect him to agree with my view about this.

From our discussions it is clear to me that you appreciate fully the implications of this being the explanation for Glyn's behaviour. I think that already you have some clear ideas what you could do about this, including getting Roy and Glyn's father helping you in being the 'boss'.

As we agreed, I will see you in eight weeks time when we can review how matters are progressing.

In this letter it is worth noting the comment about Glyn not agreeing; it is useful to include such a statement if the parent has a tendency to inappropriately ask a child for their view. This predicts the disagreement and implicitly places the child in the most helpful position for adults to assist and manage their development.

Action Expectors

The consultant offers the action expector the opportunity to explore the ideology that leads to their expectation that the consultant will take responsibility for the next step in the search for a solution (see Models of Helping, p. 137).

As we have seen, for many action expectors there is a process of discovery of their own agency in dealing with the problem they present. This occurs because the referral process erroneously prepared the client to expect that the consultant will actually do something and that their role is one of relatively passive recipients of this service. As the interview unfolds, however, they envisage solutions within the realms of their own responsibility. With other clients, however, there is a firm, if not rigid, ideology that the professional is indeed somebody who should and will take action on their behalf. When this occurs the nature of the boundary between professional and client should be explored within the context of talking about the consultant's role. The questions to be posed therefore would be:

- What would it feel like for you if I said that my position did not allow me to take such action?
- What would you do if, because of my professional role, I was unable to do what you ask?

In reflecting on this question there are ultimately only two possible future strategies that are open to the client.

(a) Find somebody who is likely to take this action.
(b) Go away and think again.

(a) It may well be that in a particular client context there is somebody who is better placed to provide professional support and the consultant should help the client identify such people.

> Mrs Gibson, her husband and her family care for Mrs Ward, Mrs Gibson's elderly mother who has recently suffered a stroke. The Gibson family have found that caring for Mrs Ward in her infirm state has created a number of practical problems as well as some interpersonal family stresses. This has occurred at the same time as Mr and Mrs Gibson have found it difficult getting on with their teenage son who is planning to leave home. Mrs Gibson consulted her family doctor because she was feeling depressed with the situation. The doctor referred the family to a family counsellor as she saw this as being a 'family-based problem'. Mr and Mrs Gibson attended the interview, in which the counsellor adopted a consultation approach. The couple had the expectation that the counsellor would recommend that Mrs Ward be offered a place in a residential unit; they were unsure to whom this recommendation should be made. They agreed with the counsellor that there was a family difficulty for them but they saw this as being very separate from their desire to see that Mrs Ward's situation in the family be resolved. They appreciated that the counsellor could not directly intervene in this way and they were pleased to accept a referral to a social worker who could make an assessment. Mr and Mrs Gibson said they would seek family sessions once the current situation had been dealt with.

It is in this situation that the consultant needs to be very clear about his/her position in the helping/professional context. Such clarity ensures that appropriate boundaries are kept and the professional only takes on and discusses work relevant to the mandate given to him/her by the agency and by the context. Certainly the consultant should be clear that brief consultation work is mandated by his/her agency for the particular difficulties that typically present. This clarity then defines a boundary, setting the limit for what the consultant can undertake in practice. For example, our consultant dealing with Mr and Mrs Gibson was asked to make a recommendation which was beyond the brief of her job and indeed her professional expertise. The consultant has the role of a family counsellor in a particular context. She is not a professional who can make assessments about the need for residential care in the elderly. The boundary of the role hence determines the action that can be taken and the consultation process requires that this boundary is respected continually.

Problems ensue when consultants neglect their own role boundary and attempt action that is outside of it. Consultants should be mindful of this because they are individuals who enter the caring professions to help others, a desire that can often prevent clarity of thought about what can and cannot be done under particular circumstances.

(b) The second strategy is necessary when the consultant says that their position prevents some action and the client simply has to think again. In the usual way of sitting with and reflecting on a client's thoughts and feelings, the consultant may be required to explore with the client the very issue of the consultant's inability to comply with the client's expectations. This raises an important point in the consultation process in that the consultant may expect that consultation will have a final result, a discernible outcome. However, this is not the case. The actual contribution the consultant makes to the client is to simply add to the unfolding elements of the life story of the client. With action expectors and opinion seekers, the consultant may be able to see and take part in that process of discovery. This is not necessarily the case for all clients as some will come, have the experience of feeling heard, but will become aware in an openly discussed fashion that the consultant cannot and does not meet the client's expectations. We will see later how communications are made to the client about this situation. However, at this stage consultants should be clear that not being able to meet a client's expectations, when discussed in an open, non-conflictual manner, can ultimately prove just as beneficial to clients as the process of directly being able to fully satisfy client expectations.

For clients whose expectations cannot be met the consultation statement will therefore reflect how the clients are dealing with this very situation. The statement needs to raise the possibility that the action the client perceives as diminishing, if not removing their difficulty in the future is in fact only one of several potential solutions. This is achieved by outlining in a clear way the client's ideology about the action that is required and then contrasting it with the activity that the consultant is 'permitted' to undertake in his/her role. The consultation statement should therefore contain:

- an outline of the client's ideology that leads to their expectation of the consultant;
- the client's expectation of the outcome of the action taken by the consultant and how this will solve the problem;
- a brief outline of the consultant's professional role in this situation;
- potential alternative strategies for having someone else take the desired action;
- potential alternative strategies for dealing with the fundamental problem;
- future action by the consultant *vis-à-vis* the client.

The last two elements might not be included if the client had a view which saw the expected action as being the only solution to the problem.

In providing the consultation statement the developmental focus is included at the beginning. However, with action expectors, particularly those who rigidly hold onto that position, this element of the statement would not be included in a letter if it be deemed that one should be sent. In our experience it is preferable to omit the placing of the problem into its developmental context and on some occasions the outline of the client's ideology about the consultation should also be left out. This is done as clients with this perspective, although they willingly see the importance of the broad context in the face-to-face situation, find it more intrusive when they reflect on it as written words a few days later. When clients have a firm definite focus on their expectations of actions, any other elements introduced by the consultant are quite quickly eroded following the interview. The client's view is therefore concentrated on the 'conflict' between what he/she expects and what the consultant is able to provide and this is what needs to be reflected in the letter.

As the consultant is very clear about what is and what is not possible, the client therefore has to reflect on the means by which they can then achieve their goal. A letter which therefore focuses on the impasse orientates clients to consider what change of tack is necessary for themselves.

The example letter that follows is designed for a client with a very clear view of the action he expected.

> Brian is a 25-year-old man with a job as an administrative assistant in a large company. He has a stammer which is marked on occasions. He lives at home with his parents, both of whom are retired. He has virtually no social contacts outside of the family. The parents and Brian go out together and take holidays together. Brian's older married sister keeps telling him that he should have an independent life. His parents indicate occasionally that he should do something about his stammer. Brian went to see his doctor about a minor physical problem and eventually ended up discussing his situation. His doctor referred him to a speech therapist for a general assessment. Her contact with Brian resulted in the following letter.

Dear Brian,

It was pleasing to meet you the other day and I felt that we had a good discussion about the problems you face. We identified as issues the fact that you did not go out very much with your own age group, that you felt you were spending too much time at home with your parents and that your stammer was a problem to you.

I understand that your doctor in discussing this with you thought you may need some assistance with these difficulties and he referred you to me in the first instance as he wondered whether a speech therapist would be the place to start.

It was very clear from our conversation that you see your central problem being a lack of a good social life. If this improved you would expect that you would then be less tied to your parents. You would also expect that you would become much more confident and this would then lead to your stammer improving.

You were pleased that your doctor sent you along to see someone and you were hoping and expecting that whoever you saw would help you organize some social activities for yourself and perhaps even make some introductions. As you said you feel you just need help to 'get you going' and certainly this is a good plan.

In my role as a speech therapist I do help people think about their social activity but this is always in relation to their social skills, particularly as it affects their speech difficulty. For me in my job, these two things always go together. I am not able to have one without the other. At this time therefore I am not able to help you in the way you would like.

As we discussed you could talk to the social club secretary at your place of work or someone involved in community activities at your local church. These people may have a lot of practical ideas about how you could develop your social life.

Although I am unable to help you at this time you now know the kinds of ways that I look at these problems. It may well be that I can be of some assistance at a later time. If you feel I can help please do not hesitate to contact me.

This example also illustrates how with action expectors it is not necessary to organize a follow-up appointment. The nature of the contract that develops – or does not develop – between the consultant and client does not require it. However, it is always left open that the client could recontact at a later date on the understanding that the consultant works within certain boundaries and with particular sets of expectations.

An example of this nature has also been included as it demonstrates how a professional can adapt the process of consultation to a particular set of circumstances. Here the speech therapist may have believed that she was setting out to assess an individual before the offer of a therapeutic contract. Although some elements of the consultation approach would have been included in that assessment it could have been that the process would not have been described as one of consultation. However, as the interview proceeded the speech therapist became aware of Brian's expectations she subtly changed her orientation to one of consultation so that the eventual outcome emerged as it did.

Counselling Clients

Clients who have the expectation that the consultant will talk to them in a manner that helps resolve their difficulties fall into two broad categories.

1. Those clients who experience the first and second consultation interview and the offer of a follow-up as being a package that directly meets their needs.
2. Those clients who wish to have a number of sessions of counselling.

In some respects the orientation of the consultant will determine whether a client falls into category one or two. Many consultants will view the consultation process as being a service formulated in a set manner. The counselling clients of these consultants will soon appreciate that this is what is on offer and amend their expectations accordingly. Some counsellors may perceive the consultation process as being a means of assessing or gatekeeping for more typical counselling sessions. Again their counselling clients will soon perceive the 'rules' and collaborate with the consultant to establish this form of contract. It is possible for a consultant to have a position that regular counselling is not an activity that he carries out and that the client should be referred elsewhere if this is what is expected.

With those clients for whom the consultation package meets their counselling needs the consultation statement should

- identify all the issues discussed and highlight some changes of perception or feeling that the client reported on during the interviews;
- indicate issues, themes or decisions that have arisen but are not resolved so that the client is directed toward certain aspects of the presenting problem before the follow-up appointment;
- identify issues that could be reviewed at the follow-up session.

> Ms Makone is a 25-year-old woman of Asian ethnic background. She has referred herself to the counselling service provided by her employers. In the first session she described herself as 'basically depressed and struggling to make a life for myself'. After two consultation contacts she decided she had some new ideas on her situation.

Dear Ms Makone

I was pleased to meet with you on the two occasions that we did to discuss the difficulties you have been facing. As I promised I am writing down a summary of our conversation so that you can use it as an aide-mémoire over the next couple of weeks. Although our discussion shifted from topic to topic, I find the best way of putting these things down is in terms of the way the story unfolds.

We discussed how you left home to go to university and when you finished you returned to live with your parents. Your feelings about these moves were that you wished to move away from home but found it difficult particularly because of your mother's attitude to your doing things independently. There was a time when you returned home when you had the same depressed feelings and anxious moments that you have had now. With the help of a friend you eventually found a place of your own and you now have your own flat. You felt that your older sister could have helped you with your move at that time but unfortunately she did not. You gave me the impression that you felt your sister has been content to allow you to deal with your parents as it then means that she does not have to do too much work with them herself.

When you were living in your flat the situation did seem to improve for you and you felt somewhat better. Unfortunately your father died suddenly and unexpectedly about 18 months ago and you are aware that it took you a long time to feel you were coping with this loss. Again, my impression is that although you are still grieving for your father you no longer feel overwhelmed by your feelings. You have been very worried since his death about how much you should help your mother and the way in which you should do this. It did seem as though what you wish is to have a situation where your mother does not dictate to you how you should run your life.

With this as the background, you have felt yourself recently to be depressed and miserable for some time and within the last six months you have found once again that you have been anxious about going out and meeting people. As we talked about your difficulties, it did seem to me that we were talking about how people try to leave home in a good way. We talked about how many people think of leaving home starting at 18 and then finishing completely by the time they are 21. Unfortunately as you and I know, life is never as simple as this. Leaving home is a process that continues for many years, well into the 20s and beyond for a great many people. Everyone faces a number of ordinary difficulties with this step. My feeling is that this is certainly the case for yourself, particularly as you have had to contend with some family members not being helpful to you and the loss of your father.

In our conversations it did seem to me that you were becoming aware that the difficulties you face have not just followed on from the death of your Dad, but have some root in how things were earlier. I also thought that you have been hoping that other family members would try to put things right for you rather than you making your own efforts to organize your life for yourself.

We agreed that you would be considering ways in which you could see some of your time as being for you and your family, some for you and your friends from work and some for just you. We also thought that it would be a good idea for you to keep a check on how much energy you were able to put into these three different types of activities. As I told you, I do not think this is a situation of you trying hard to get over this, but merely seeing where you place your energy when you feel you have some.

When we next meet in 6 weeks time, we will review how your time allocation is going. We will also review how depressed you have been feeling generally and if you feel that it is no better then we will discuss whether you feel that you need some medical help for this. No doubt you will be thinking about all the things we have discussed and our next meeting will be an opportunity to see whether you feel you have got on with that.

I look forward to the next time we do meet.

With clients who expect to have a number of counselling sessions a valuable question is:

• What would indicate that things are improving for you?

For these clients the statement will include:

• those issues, themes to be discussed in sessions;
• the number of sessions agreed in the first instance;
• the way the number of sessions is altered – increased or stopped;
• signs that the client will identify as pointing toward an improvement in their situation.

Should the consultant choose to be in a professional role that does not offer counselling as an on-going activity, the consultation statement should include

• those themes and issues the client could take to a counsellor;
• indications that counselling is no longer required;
• action that the consultant intends to take to assist the client in finding a counsellor for themselves.

Mr Milne was 56 years of age, his wife was six years his junior. They had two children who had both married and moved out of the area. Mr Milne had worked in a middle-ranking job in the Civil Service. His office was relocated some distance away and he was identified as being a person who could take early retirement. Mr Milne was anxious about this and through the personnel office arranged to see a consultant. The consultation letter follows.

Dear Mr Milne,

Following our two discussions I am writing with my views on the situation and to outline what we agreed.

As we noted you and your wife are in that time of life when the children are living some distance from home and your extended family is now very dispersed and indeed some of them have passed away. Consequently you and your wife have, in a natural way, less to do with family affairs than you once did. This has happened at a time when you and she would be closely making plans for how you will deal with retirement and again, the natural way of things would be to prepare for this in your own way at your own pace.

Unfortunately circumstances have meant that you have been unable to get ready for the next phase of life in your own time because the situation dictates that you will retire very shortly. Because of these things you have felt very let down by your employers and you still feel angry with the speed at which this is being foisted on you.

You are also aware that in a number of respects you have felt somewhat abandoned by some family members in that they have moved away. This is the case even though they keep in touch with you.

You are clearly very uncertain what to do with your retirement time, particularly as it may involve you in being retired for possibly ten years before your wife is able to join you. As you had always imagined your retirement to be something you and she embarked on together, you are unsure as to what it will be like doing it 'on your own'.

As we discussed the situation, you became aware that the mixture of negative feelings was making you look on retirement as being an insurmountable barrier rather than a problem to solve.

Your clear expectation, and one that your wife originally inspired, is that if you could talk through some of your feelings and thoughts you might then be able to consider afresh what is ahead of you. I feel this is a very good idea and I am more than willing to help you with this.

We agreed that we would meet on six further occasions when we would discuss your feelings about how the matter has been handled given your length of service, we would talk about family issues, particularly those relevant to working out a new relationship with your children and re-establishing your relationship with your sister now she is a widow. We also agreed to discuss how you and your wife may set about organizing life with you at home and she at work and as we both acknowledged, that may involve discussion of roles in your marriage.

We will review how matters are progressing at the sixth session. Before then, should you feel less angry and more involved in the practical issues of retiring – organizing finances, planning activities etc., you will let me know and we will review matters at that point.

I am pleased we will be meeting in this way and I look forward to working with you. See you on the 24th at 2.30 pm.

Reluctant Clients

Reluctance is not something that resides within a person. It is not a personality trait. It merely recognizes that individuals differ in the degree to which they are motivated to undertake a particular activity. What is recognized from a systemic viewpoint is that if the context were changed then the client might have more desire to be involved in a previously avoided activity. Typically what happens when some reluctance is found within a context is that an individual is aware that to follow one activity will automatically result in a conflict with something else they desire. The presence of conflict of thoughts and feelings, i.e. ambivalence, is undoubtedly an underlying feature of the context where reluctance occurs. The clients we are particularly concerned with are those who come along because they have been 'sent', and who will have as their priority the maintenance of their relationship with the referrer rather than the construction of an involvement with the consultant.

The ambivalence involved in this situation is that the client has a particular set of expectations of the referrer that does not involve consultation and/or counselling being seen as necessary but their expectations do include that they will undertake what the referrer suggests in order to maintain the hope that the referrer will eventually meet all their expectations. The way in which this occurs is different in different contexts and hence 'reluctance' can only be fully appreciated within terms of the system in which the referrer and consultant relate. Different contexts throw up different problems.

- A single-parent young mother who attends her appointment with a psychologist for help with her young son's behaviour because the social worker has sent her. Her ambivalence is based around her desire to conform with the social worker's wishes because she fears that if she does not her child may be removed.
- A man with a number of personal and marital difficulties who enjoys and benefits from his visits to his female doctor. When she refers him to a counsellor he attends because he wishes to please his doctor but does not wish to transfer his loyalty to another person.
- A man who sometimes drinks a great deal, such that it comes to the attention of his employers. His line manager suggests that he 'go for counselling'. To maintain his position with his employers he sees the counsellor but he does not believe he has a problem.
- A woman who, on several occasions, reports to her doctor that her son is a problem as a means of alluding to her criticism of her husband. The family doctor refers her to a child specialist as he perceives this to be

the principal problem. The woman, however, had wished her doctor to deal with her husband and only attended for the other professional as she did not wish to be seen as being an uninterested mother.

When faced with clients with such dilemmas the consultant will follow the general process of the consultation interview and will have asked questions concerning process of referral and linking this to how the client views possible outcomes. The consultant then has to determine whether the role he occupies is one where the client is only seen once or where more than one contact could be possible. For those contexts in which one meeting would be appropriate, the consultant determines whether or not it is feasible for him to consider the referrer as the 'customer'. Should this be the case then he will frame a statement which will correspond with what has been said by the client and which meets the requirements of the referrer–consultant relationship. The client would receive this statement in the interview and then both client and referrer would receive the written version. For these situations the statement would follow the general pattern that has been outlined principally providing a brief summary of the client's ideology of the problem. In these circumstances it would not be appropriate to offer an ideology of the consultation process as it would be too direct a comment about the workings of the referrer–client relationship. To do this would involve contributing to an unhelpful triangular relationship.

> An example of this client group is demonstrated with the situation of Mr Kolne who enjoyed talking about his difficulties with his female doctor. At their meeting the consultant and Mr Kolne agreed that the consultant would write directly to the doctor with a copy to Mr Kolne.

Dear Dr Williams,

Thank you for asking me to see Mr Kolne. He came along to see me at my office on Friday last. We agreed that I would write to you with a summary of our discussion.

Mr Kolne is 42 years old. He and his wife Susan have been married for 14 years. They have one daughter Sophie who is nearly 11 years old. For some time Mr Kolne has been feeling rather low about how he and his wife have been getting on. He knows that occasionally he feels that his spirits are up and that he is then able to cope well. He is uncertain how things change for him but he becomes miserable and feels himself to be withdrawing from people at home and at work. When this happens he does not wish to talk to people very much but he has appreciated the support from yourself and his brother whom he sees infrequently.

Mr Kolne is aware that sometimes men of his age have a 'mid-life crisis'. He has wondered whether this applies to himself but he does not quite understand what it might mean in his circumstances. He has also hoped that his wife might be more understanding of him and he has been disappointed that she has not made very many comments about his miserable mood. Again he is uncertain how these feelings will develop and effect the situation.

Mr Kolne knows that in the past he has dealt with difficulties for himself by just 'sitting tight' and seeing them through. He anticipates that this strategy will also be useful for this current problem providing he is able to receive the support he enjoys at present.

Mr Kolne and I both feel that our consultation meeting was a beneficial one as it served to clarify the situation for himself. We have no further plans to meet.

The other category of clients are those where there is clearly a possibility that further work of a counselling nature could be offered. Clients in these situations are not only ambivalent about attending but they are also ambivalent about the 'degree' to which they have a problem. The task therefore is to validate the perception that the problem is minor, not requiring further work, whilst at the same time accepting the perception that it could nevertheless be a difficulty that would benefit from some help. The consultant therefore directly addresses the ambivalence created by these differences and offers the client alternatives in terms of what could happen next. A boundary is therefore created between the conditions under which on-going work could be taken on by the consultant and conditions under which the client would not seek help. This orientates the client to those issues that will determine how the next step is to be undertaken by themselves. The example of this work is provided by Mrs Scott, the lady who complained about her son's behaviour as a means of alluding to her critical feelings about her husband.

Dear Mrs Scott,

It was good to meet you and Gary the other day and I was pleased that we could discuss the problems so freely. As I promised, I am writing you a summary of our meetings so that you can consider the best way to proceed.

From what you told me, Gary is a boy who sometimes can be good and sometimes bad. When he is good he is well-mannered and loving but when bad, he can sneer at you, not do as he is told, be spiteful towards his sister and be rather arrogant. It does seem that he has difficulties with friends. Some of this is unfortunately due to the action of other people and some of it due to his own attitude.

As we discussed Gary is approaching early adolescence and at this time of life, some boys emphasize their good points whilst others emphasize their bad points. As you know it is impossible to tell which boy will do what, but you know you have to be watchful of this so you can offer the correct amount of parental advice, guidance and discipline when needed.

When children have difficulties, there can be many causes and sometimes there is just one. I know that you feel that if Mr Scott could spend more time with Gary then it would make a very important difference. As I have not met your husband I do not know what he thinks but from what you tell me there is an obvious problem in his being able to arrange his work so that he is more available for you and the children.

Under the circumstances I feel that we can do one of three things:

1. *If you feel that Gary has a behaviour problem that has to be dealt with then I am more than willing to see you to offer advice.*
2. *If you feel that there is a problem and that its cause is how you and your husband are jointly dealing with things then I am quite willing to see you as a family.*
3. *If you feel that the problem is not really a serious one and that time will make a difference then I would be pleased to leave matters to your judgement.*

For the present we have not made any further arrangements for an appointment but should you wish to see me again I would be happy to meet with you to see how you look on these alternatives.

Once the consultation statement has been made the remaining task in the initial interview is to arrange the follow-up. This is discussed in the next chapter.

6

ORGANIZING THE FOLLOW-UP SESSION

SETTING UP THE MEETING

Once the consultation statement has been made and the arrangements concerning the sending of the consultation letter discussed, the consultant then needs to turn to the issue of the follow-up appointment. As stressed earlier this appointment is mentioned at the beginning of the interview session as being a possibility. It is cast as an appointment which in one sense is outside of the consultation whilst being integral to the whole process. The consultation statement brings to an end the actual consultation in that the client attended, told his story and the consultant responded. The follow-up session is definitely not a part of the consultant's response to the presenting problem. It is however the opportunity to cooperatively evaluate the effect of the consultation with the clients.

The follow-up session is not always wanted or required and clients need to be given the choice of whether or not they wish to meet the consultant for a follow-up. The important point is that the client is made aware that another meeting can occur if they request it. This places the control of the process firmly in the hands of the client. It also serves to plant the seeds of the consultant's 'ghost' with them. This is the on-going imaginary relationship the client has with the consultant into the future, which the client will construct using information from the experience of meeting the consultant.

- Most people find it useful to come back for a follow-up to see how things are going – a means of you working out how things are progressing. Would you like us to arrange a further meeting?

Clients with whom matters have seemingly been straightforward most frequently respond that they do not wish to have a follow-up. The consultant, depending on the work context, can suggest that they contact the consultant within a period of time, say 3–8 months, just to let the consultant know how things are going.

- I would appreciate knowing how things are going so perhaps you could call to let me know. If you can't get me on the 'phone please leave a message with our administrative staff.

This approach allows the client to time when the contact will be made. There is a clear indication that it will not be a person-to-person contact and this permits the client to determine the exact nature of what will be said. Importantly it also permits the call not to be made as there is no personal expectation from the consultant to speak with the client.

Many clients choose to have a follow-up and within certain guidelines they should determine the length of time between meetings. Any meeting which is less than six weeks away is simply a follow-on appointment, i.e. it is an appointment in which the two meetings are linked too closely together. A very short time gap does not allow clients to leave the consultation, reconstruct it in their own context, put their new information into effect and then evaluate the outcome of all that. Similarly too long a time-gap creates too much of a space between the consultation and a discussion about it. Therefore for any context, and even for particular client expectations within that context, there are minimal and maximal periods for organizing the follow-up. Our experience is that a follow-up between 6 and 14 weeks is most suitable, with 8–10 weeks as the most frequent optimal period. These times are however only guidelines as clients have their own way of considering the passage of time. In different circumstances, the time frame of the follow-up can be built around family holidays, term times, dates of performance evaluations at work, Christmas and Easter breaks, visits of relatives from afar, attendance at courses etc. For each client, time will be organized differently and this needs to be borne in mind when setting the timing and time span of the follow-up. Consultants should be prepared for clients cancelling follow-up sessions when they believe it is 'not needed'. A brief letter leaving it open if they wish to return in the future is all that is required in these circumstances.

With our examples, Mr and Mrs Dean felt that a six-week follow-up was suitable. They had sought advice and gone away with some clear practical steps they could take. A shorter time span was therefore appropriate.

Mr Hooper on the other hand was uncertain if he wished to have a follow-up as he was aware of how he might proceed but not of how quickly things might occur. This was particularly relevant as he clearly wished to report on the conclusion of something to the consultant. As Mr Hooper was to have his work section reviewed in some four months time, the consultant suggested that he contact him in 10–12 weeks to let him know if it would be helpful to arrange a follow-up.

Some clients indicate that they want a much longer period before their follow-up session; should this be longer than the 3–4 months maximum period, the consultant should not make an appointment there and then. The client should be given the responsibility to contact the consultant to make an appointment nearer the time.

In all cases where clients are left with the responsibility of contacting the consultant, they should know that it is the consultant's practice to write a simple enquiry letter after 6 months. This is to ensure that there is some reminder to the client that the consultation took place. A query letter can then serve the purpose of stimulating the client's reflection once again on their consultation and their response to it. Our query letter is brief and simple and is laid out in full below.

Dear Mr and Mrs Smith

As I promised when we met last June I am writing to you as I have been wondering how things are going for you and your family. Please feel free to contact me if you wuld like to meet.

The majority of these letters go unanswered, a proportion of clients reply that things are going well and a smaller number respond to the letter by seeking an appointment. At one time we considered the proportion of unanswered letters to be an indication of some dissatisfaction, but our evaluation research does not suggest this. It would appear that many clients were satisfied with the contact and felt no need to respond in any way.

CONDUCTING THE FOLLOW-UP SESSION

In the follow-up session the consultant needs to bear in mind that the original interviews were conducted around the 'agreed' problem. This is the point of reference for those interviews and for this interview also. Similarly it cannot be neglected that a consultation took place and that the consultant made a particular response. The response is also therefore a reference point for the follow-up session. If a letter has been sent then the consultant can assume that he and the clients agreed on the content of that letter initially and this means there was general agreement on the consultant's verbal statement. The letter will therefore provide the framework for the follow-up discussion. However, if for some reason a consultation letter has not been sent the consultant has to seek out the meaning the clients placed on the verbal statement for sometimes clients' understanding and memory can be at odds with the memory and understanding of the consultant. We have had experiences of clients reporting how beneficial they found the consultation and then reported their memory of our statements which were almost diametrically opposed to our own memory and written notes recorded at the time! As always the consultant operates within the clients' frame of reference.

The follow-up appointment begins with:

- How are things?

The replies to this question are dealt with in the usual manner of reflecting and summarizing. The consultant will be seeking to highlight those problems, actions, words, ideas, etc., that were mentioned in the original interviews. From our ongoing examples Mr and Mrs Dean reported that things were going much better for them as they had developed a system for dealing with the end of the day and it appeared to be working. Although Jamie was still difficult they felt they were coping with him much more ably. The consultant then seeks to contrast the current situation with that which existed just prior to the time of the first interview. This is done so that the difference can be explored in terms of changed actions and changed ideas.

- What is different about now and when I first saw you?
- Are you doing anything different?
- Compared to when we first met, what do you feel has changed 'naturally' and what have you set about changing?

Mrs Dean reported that she deliberately put time aside to work out what needed to be done. She was aware that she mainly did it on her own but she felt pleased that her husband then agreed with her plan. Mr Dean thought that he was trying hard to be involved in the planning but he was happy to follow the plan that was set. They both thought that even though they were tired and that life itself was sometimes a chore, they had a means of dealing with it.

The consultant should place such changes within the context of the consultation, particularly in terms of the relationship between himself and the client.

- Given what we discussed originally, was there anything that I said or did that was useful/helpful?

It is at this point that the client reports on the usefulness or otherwise of the consultant's statements and this may well appear different to what the consultant would have considered as being useful. It needs to be remembered that the consultant is in some ways only a brief companion as the client makes his/her changes and all of these changes are potentialities with or without the intervention of the consultant. Therefore a client's explanation of following some pattern of changed behaviour that is already within his/her repertoire may bear little relation to the intention behind the suggestions that were made. The consultant has no intention of 'correcting' any report or of being clear about what may or may not have been said. A strictly pragmatic approach to the outcome is what is required: one that signifies the client's satisfaction with what has happened, rather than a search for some undefinable key ingredient. Mr Dean reported that he had found it most helpful when the consultant told them that they were an ordinary couple with an ordinary problem. He had been afraid there was something seriously wrong and he was pleased to be told that every family met such difficulties. Mrs Dean said that it had been helpful thinking about what to do about Jamie, but she had really benefited from finding out that she had not been organizing things very well when she believed that she was in fact an organized person. When the consultant quizzically commented on not remembering that piece of the discussion, Mrs Dean told him that was because they had not discussed it. These were her thoughts afterwards. Here we see the power of self-reflection when an empathic questioning style of interviewing is adopted.

When Mr Hooper attended for his follow-up he reported that he had found the consultation helpful as it had helped him to think about the way things were linked together. In particular he had become aware that his wish to deal with home, work and his relationship as separate issues was not possible. He now believed there was an underlying central problem and that was how he felt about himself and his job. He knew at the time of the consultation that he needed to think about things differently but he was unsure how. Then unexpectedly a job became available in a rival company and it was suggested to him that he should apply. Mr Hooper's greatest recollection of the consultation interview was that of talking about being courageous and somebody telling him he had a good understanding of his situation which was obviously difficult. He decided to apply for this job and he got it. So now he was about to start working for a new firm and he felt very positive about this. He was still in his relationship with Ms King but he felt more in control of it as it was now moving further away from work. He was aware that Ms King had some long-term hopes for the relationship that he did not share but at the moment he did not wish to do anything about this. He was also aware that another woman he knew had indicated that she would like to go out with him; he was pleased he did not do anything about this. Mr Hooper felt that the decision he now faced was the one concerning his wife. A bit of him wanted to leave and some of him wanted to stay because of his relationship with his children. He was uncertain about this. Mr Hooper did not wish any further contact with the consultant.

For these clients, as indeed for every client, it is important to cast these changes into developmental family life-cycle terms. Mr and Mrs Dean have faced a typical life-cycle transition as the wife/mother takes on a working role outside of the home. This involves adaptations and adjustments that are often only created through a 'crisis' process where matters appear to be very problematic and unresolved before an acceptable solution is established. Mr Hooper has found himself in a position where he needs to make some decisions about the nature of his commitment to his long-term relationship with his wife, his relationship with Ms King and to himself. The realization that, to a considerable extent, we shape our own destiny is one that comes to many people and for Mr Hooper it has come now. Each client, in language familiar to them, is helped by hearing his/her changes compared to a process that is familiar to many. But it is not the similarity in experiences that make them shareable, it is the ease with which individuals can empathize with the predicament of others that allows for the creation of a 'normative' occurrence. The consultant therefore should be able to make small points from this perspective as the clients recount the way they have been attempting to experience a change in their lives. The developmental perspective is not focused on strict phases; its focus is on process and change and the consultant's comments need to reflect this (see The Developmental Perspective, p. 128).

When clients have received a letter from the consultant a series of questions readily follow:

- Was my letter useful/helpful?
- What did each individual think and feel about it?
- Who read it? How many times?
- What did you say to each other after you read it?
- Did you show it to anybody? Is there anyone you might show it to?
- Reading it today, are any of the statements relevant/not relevant?

A letter more easily allows the consultant to focus on the interview as a follow-up of the original consultation. It also makes for an easier discussion about the nature of the client's interactive system as the way the letter is used by the family reveals to everyone particular interactive sequences and mechanisms. The letter in some family systems becomes the symbol of communication and the manner in which it is passed around, read out or just put into a drawer and left reveals how the family dealt with that communication. Mr and Mrs Dean, for example, both read the letter and then discussed whether Mr Dean's mother should be shown it; they decided that as the letter was addressed to them they should tell Mrs Zeta Dean about its contents and they hoped that would be sufficient. Mr Dean had read the letter once and Mrs Dean had re-read it approximately a week after receiving it. She did this to remind herself about some things to do with managing Jamie.

There are some clients for whom change has not occurred or been attempted and the follow-up therefore can become a means of discussing their orientation to the consultation statements. However, this is fully possible only when a letter has been sent, for without a letter the consultant cannot assume that the clients have a clear memory of what has been said. The existence of the letter allows the consultant to deal with the consultation statement as something that occurred 'last week' which may or may not have been responded to. This can be an opportunity for the consultant to discuss the nature of the relationship between the client and consultation safely at one step removed. ('That was what was said then, I'm not sure what is being said here now.') The centrality or peripherality of the consultation to the client is therefore clearly revealed by this type of discussion and the consultant can then orientate or even re-orientate himself to the position the client now occupies in the readiness to change cycle.

As the consultant is constantly operating from the perspective that change and difference are a natural part of life, he needs to ensure that the clients do not look on the statement or letter as being placed in tablets of stone. The questions during follow-up should maintain this perspective:

- Which bits of the statement/letter do you think we could change today?
- In three or six months time which bits do you think we could change?

Nearly all clients respond to these questions in terms of the section of the statement where advice, opinion, theory etc., were offered. This is because this section is seen as what they came for and it is seen as coming from the consultant personally. The narrative/historical section tends to be viewed as being that 'which is already known'. Though, as we have seen, this may have been constructed jointly just as much as the advice or opinion. Should clients talk about the need to change some of the 'story' elements; this would indicate either that the consultant made too many assumptions about this aspect and therefore played too strong a role in the narrative construction or that the client is undergoing a process of considerable change, such that the whole story needs to be rewritten. Whichever is the case it is only by humbly asking questions about how the consultant came to be suggesting another version of the story that matters can be clarified.

- How is it that I got the wrong end of the stick about your story?
- Did I get it wrong at the beginning or has thinking about it changed how you see it?

Many clients return for the follow-up session still encountering the same difficulty or even experiencing a new one. The consultant will then need to focus on the definition and meaning of the problem for the client. Old problems can be seen as being just a continuation of what existed before or they can be perceived in a different way with new definitions and meaning attached to them. New problems for some clients will be perceived as just another series of events that express a basic original difficulty or they can be new in circumstances, perceptions and meaning. The consultant's questioning should not imply 'if it's the same it must be the same', 'if it's different it must be new'. The client will determine the meaning of what is occurring. Should a problem (old or new) be present then the consultant will, by his questioning, imply that a new process of considering a problem is under way:

- Have you thought what you would like to do about this problem?

The responsibility for the difficulty rests with the client and the consultant should be mindful of completing one process of consultation before embarking on another.

- In dealing with the difficulty, have you thought if I may be able to help in any way?

When difficulties continue to exist, the consultant should by questioning and repeating some elements of the statements recap the process and the content of the enquiry that he and the client followed during the consultation interviews. This serves to maintain the link between the interviews as well as identifying any particular area where something was misunderstood or some action not taken. It does happen that clients readily accept and agree with some advice, opinion or explanation offered and then choose not to take action on it. These instances need to be made apparent to ensure that both client and consultant are aware of the response to what was offered. Some clients are undoubtedly greatly helped by being clear about what they would like to do but which they are choosing not to do.

Mrs Mallory was referred via her employer assistance programme because she had reported to the company doctor that her drinking was increasing. At the consultation interviews Mrs Mallory reported her drinking as being the only problem she faced. She expected and hoped that the consultant would give her an opinion about the best way to tackle the problem. The opinion that was formed was that Mrs Mallory may find it helpful to seek the assistance of her husband in dealing with her drinking and that contacting Alcoholics Anonymous may also be useful. At the follow-up which occurred two months later Mrs Mallory reported that her drinking was continuing at the same level and that although she had appreciated the consultant's opinion as helpful, she had not taken action on it. She also reported that she now felt that her relationship with her husband was not good and for the first time she was 'wondering out loud' whether her marital dissatisfaction was causing her drinking. She had realized this more fully when she had thought about seeking his help for her drinking as she had seen this as resulting in further difficulty. She felt generally that he was not supportive of her. The consultant wondered how this had not been apparent during the initial consultation meeting and Mrs Mallory believed that it was because she had become clearer about it in her own mind. Mrs Mallory was uncertain what she wished to do about this problem but she said to the consultant, 'I know that if I ask you for your opinion about it you would say I need to face up to it in some way'. Mrs Mallory left the follow-up session saying that she knew what the next steps were but at the moment she felt she should take her time in deciding how she would tackle these problems. The consultant considered that Mrs Mallory was in the contemplation stage of readiness to change, and he finished by saying 'Well that sounds like a good strategy but I guess you will have to consider that in terms of what you have called the damage drinking is causing to your body and your relationships.' Mrs Mallory replied 'That's the dilemma I have to struggle with for a while.'

Consultants should complete the follow-up interview with a simple recap of the expectations the client came with and how that was met. A good introduction to the résumé is 'This is the question you came with and this is how we answered it'. The consultant and the client need to remind themselves that the consultation process in terms of the client's life is just a minor sub-plot. In this sub-plot a problem or query is raised, a response is made and the client then takes responsibility in terms of any action taken as a result of the response. It is in the client's interests that a process of repetition of consultation is avoided. The consultation process cannot continue by addressing the same presenting problem; one discussion about the problem defines the limits of the process and that implies that there is a beginning and an end to that process.

As the consultation has set about following a course of interaction which is based on the client's frame of reference, the client toward its end can come to appreciate that what has occurred has been predicated upon his or her own assumptions. As this occurs in a non-attached, empathic manner, the client can then feel empowered to confront those issues and problems that had seemed overwhelming and unmoving. It is at this point that many clients report, 'I think I was expecting you to do something with your magic wand but I know if I face this in my own way it will be dealt with.' When clients appreciate their own agency then clearly there is no danger in suggesting that at some point in the future they may need consultation again. Consultants, however, need to be mindful of ensuring that the relationships with all clients are based on the limits of the consultation approach and the consultant's activity within that approach.

Another problem may be raised which if different to the first one could be deserving of another consultation. To address this new problem would require another appointment. For those clients who clearly need to return, the time of the next consultation interview should depend on an evaluation of the degree and nature of change that has occurred. It is in the way a consultant deals with the new set of appointments that another straightforward repetition of the consultation interview is avoided. The consultation process is not a response to the 'emergency' of any situation and hence the message that the matter can be dealt with in a serious but non-urgent manner is the one to be given. There should be a space of reasonable length to a new consultation (6–8 weeks) and as so many of the preliminaries have been dealt with, that consultation should be possibly undertaken in one session. The client should be informed of this at the time so as to specify the time boundaries within which the consultant operates. Most counselling contexts can safely operate on the basis that per referral a maximum of two consultations following one after the other is the limit. In our experience it is not helpful to arrange more than one other consultation as to do so would be to allow the approach to drift into a 'therapy' type of approach. If clients appear to be requesting more than this then the consultant should seek supervision. Of course in many contexts some clients may seek a re-referral after a period of time and this is to be expected in the process of consultation. Our practice, following a first consultation, is to ensure that the process reaches some clearly denoted conclusion at the end of the follow-up and then inform the client that they can contact the consultant if they wish to see him again. This again places the responsibility with the client. It retains the relationship of the client 'engaging' the consultant for a professional service.

Clients who re-present for consultation in a period less than six months generally do so with the same problem but with some alteration in their position in the readiness to change cycle. In these cases the consultant can conduct the interview as an amended follow-up. With clients who re-present in a period of greater than six months there will generally have been a number of changes, in life events, in perception and in presenting problem. In these situations the consultation process should be done afresh though some short-cuts can be made by the consultant agreeing 'what is known'. For many of these clients it is the speed of the changes in their lives that they come to appreciate and once this is fully in their awareness, their own manner of problem-solving becomes primary.

In order to bring the process to a conclusion, the consultant therefore needs to:

1. maintain a focus on the problem as set by the client;
2. maintain an approach within the language of the client's expectations;
3. identify differences in behaviour, attitude, perception, between the initial consultation and the follow-up interview;
4. place the responsibility for the evaluation of these changes with the client;
5. place the responsibility for determining future action with the client;
6. maintain the boundaries of the consultation process.

THEORETICAL FOUNDATIONS

In this chapter we present the theoretical underpinings to our practice of therapeutic consultation. As we outlined in the first chapter some of these ideas were active in our thinking from the outset. Some ideas we came across in the process of the model's development and were instrumental in our changing elements of the approach. Other ideas we have found or come to understand anew since the model has acquired its stable state. In the clinical discovery of this approach ideas and theories have principally followed practice and experience, with that practice grounded in the common ideology of the counselling and therapy fields. The presentation of these ideas does not require that they be read in sequence; from the last to the first is just as valid as the first to last. Indeed these ideas are so interlinked can be approached in any order and linked to the preceding chapters in any way.

THE SOCIAL CONSTRUCTIONIST VIEW OF THE COUNSELLOR–CLIENT RELATIONSHIP

Social constructionism is a perspective rooted in what is termed the 'post-modern' tradition. This is a tradition in stark contrast to the philosophical and ideological perspective that ushered in the beginning of the twentieth century. Modernism assumes that individuals are inherently rational in their thinking and behaviour. The ability to reason together with a careful and systematic observation of the 'world' will lead to the uncovering of 'basic structures' and the discovery of the 'real', 'final', and ultimately 'true' version of the world. The desire for accurate and true descriptions of the world represents the defining goals of modernism with empirical science being seen as the principal and most sophisticated system for making and evaluating progress towards the final goal. Modernist therapies regard the task as being to help the client talk through problems and difficulties in a rational and objective manner. The form and direction of therapy is dictated by the instruments and apparatus of rationality and objectivity, namely research evidence, formal measurements of change, and outcome measurements. The focus is upon 'things' and the goal remains truth directed.

The social sciences in general and the psychotherapies as a specific, applied example are entering a period of traumatic revision where basic philosophical foundations are under challenge from a post-modern perspective. A *social constructionist* view is emerging which questions any framework suggesting that social entities such as individuals, families and groups have a stability and an internal definable structure. It is a view that questions whether anything is objectively knowable. Social constructionism is therefore an epistemological perspective which takes issue with the modernist/structuralist idea that a real world exists that can be known with objective certainty and can ultimately be summarized in unchallengeable truth statements. Social constructionism, in contrast to this pursuit of final truths, regards ideas, knowledge, memories, etc. as arising from social interaction and as being mediated through language. All social knowledge, it is suggested, evolves in conversations and dialogues people have with one another. It is through the ongoing conversation with intimates that the individual develops a sense of identity, a sense of their world and eventually an inner voice or dialogue.

Post-modernism has its origins in the field of semiotics and literary criticism (thus the use of analogies of stories, narratives, texts, etc.) and hence social constructionism continues to develop, influenced by ideas in literary, political, and philosophical fields of thought, e.g. Foucault (1975), and in social science research by such authors as Gergen (1991), and Harre (1984). The implications of social constructionist ideas is profound and fundamental to the practice of all forms of psychotherapy. To date it has perhaps been explored most widely in the field of family therapy. A notable exponent of this view is Hoffman (1992) who discusses the psychological foundations on which traditional psychotherapeutic practice is based and she has identified five 'sacred cows' which are under threat from the arguments of social constructionism.

1. *Objective social research.* Social constructionism not only rejects the idea of a singular truth but rejects that objective social research is possible. It argues that most of the products of objective research are based upon a constructed view of the world and its findings express one view, but a powerful view, which maintains the position of expertise and influence of a select minority.

2. *The self.* Social constructionist thinking also challenges the notion of an inner reality which can be represented by 'solid' words like cognitions, emotions, etc. The self in social constructionism does not exist within the person nor within any other social unit. Rather, the individual identity consists of an interactional history which can be arranged in a variety of patterns, depending upon the purpose and context in which, and through which, the account is being presented (see Individual Experience, p. 125).

3. *Developmental psychology.* Current psychotherapy practice is in large part based on a version of an optimal life path which, like plant life, will bear the scars of early trauma throughout life. This idea has been useful in many clinical formulations but it does not have an unquestioned status in the eyes of social constructionists. They challenge the idea that there exists any template or universal standard by which humans can measure their functioning. The ideas of chaos theory (Gleick 1987) are more in keeping with the ideas of social constructionism. Simply put, this view suggests that when a social system changes state an element of the random is always present in the process and 'outcome' of that change. Thus an event may trigger change fairly reliably in societal terms but at the individual, family and group level the outcome cannot be known. Conversely what will act as a trigger for change at these levels is also always unpredictable (see The Developmental Perspective, p. 128).

4. *The emotions.* The psychotherapies frequently subscribe to a version of repression theory, i.e. traumatic events must be emotionally relived and thereby discharged in order for the individual, the family, etc. to achieve some new position of resolution. In social constructionist terms emotions have no special status as interior states. They are viewed as yet one more aspect of communication between people and their meaning and impact will depend upon the context of their expression or description.

5. *Hierarchical levels.* Traditional psychotherapeutic theories in the use of terms and concepts, such as superficial and underlying causes, latent and manifest content, etc., reveal a belief in the hierarchical arrangement of social activity, experience and meaning. Based on the analogy of the onion ring, these theories propose that there are levels of activity which nestle one within the other and move from simple to more sophisticated, significant and hierarchically distant levels. Social constructionism would once more propose that these models are merely social inventions and that there is no reason why factors should be arranged hierarchically. Indeed this perspective questions whether there is any constant arrangement at all. It does not require a total rejection of hierarchical or any other form of arrangement but merely that such an arrangement is but one possible configuration and relationship between factors.

Within social constructionism the writings of Michel Foucault (Foucault, 1975) and particularly his ideas on the nature of 'power' have far-reaching implications for the way in which counselling is understood and practised. Foucault proposes that social power resides in the system of privileged 'discourses' that are present in any social system. The discourses themselves promote certain definitions about which persons or what topics are most important or have legitimacy in a society, e.g. scientific discourses, religious discourses, etc. All discourses in a society, Foucault argues, carry embedded assumptions which support a dominant-to-submissive relationship; the discourses of the psychotherapies are not exempt, notwithstanding how well intentioned the profession sets out to be. In particular it has been argued (Kearney et al., 1989) that the personal–social therapies have promoted the development of a professional practice which is akin to a colonial mentality, i.e. practitioners offer their skills and theories to a group designated as being in some way 'less' than the practitioners; just as the Victorian missionaries offered 'religion' to the 'primitive heathen' in the imperial colonies.

Social constructionists hold firmly to the idea that there are no incontrovertible social truths, only stories about the world that we tell ourselves and others. Therapists have a set of ideas, principles and theoretical framework (a 'story') which allows them to make assertions about how problems develop and are solved or dis-solved. Whatever the therapist's story or narrative may be, social constructionists have argued that it has privileged status in the interaction and the fact that it is usually undisclosed allows therapists to go into therapy sessions with an intervention already in mind. Then in the course of listening to the clients' account of their situation therapists develop a hypothesis that is based upon *their* narrative structure around the problem that supports their own theoretical schema. Different therapeutic approaches (or narratives) merely mean that different elements of the problem (text/story) organization and different 'levels' of the client's account are attended to. No level is more true than any other; it is just that a different type of solution to the 'problem' emerges depending on the level one is focused on. For example, some therapists may conventionally concentrate on the level of life script (e.g. Byng-Hall, 1985) while others focus on the level of behavioural episode (e.g. Minuchin, 1985). A need to consider particular levels will occur depending upon the type of solution which is mandated by the society. Thus in dealing with interpersonal abuse society requires that a behavioural episode level is utilized when the abuse is directed towards children; however, when abuse is directed towards women then other 'levels' are invoked – often unhelpful to women.

Therapies deriving from or incorporating a social constructionist perspective are inclined towards a more conversational, non-expert, collaborative engagement. They dispense with the requirement of hierarchical distinctions between client and counsellor but do not deny that the client and therapist are in distinct positions *vis-à-vis* power in the relationship. Possibly the key assumption and tenet of post-modernist practice is that the expert does *not* have a superior position from which a correct or better appraisal of the client's position can be made.

An example of this aproach is that of Goolishian and his colleagues of the Galveston Group. Goolishian and Anderson (1992), without subscribing wholly to the post-modernist position, developed a style of working in which the therapist maintains a position of 'not knowing'. This approach of respect for the client's perspective contradicts the idea of the therapist going to meet a client already having some idea of what it is the client must understand, or even must practise in order to achieve some higher, better form of life experience. Post-modern therapists do not believe that there is anything that the client 'must know'. They argue rather that knowledge, being socially arrived at, changes and renews itself in each moment of interaction. There are no prior meanings hiding in people's stories waiting to be discovered by a more learned or tutored ear. The interviewing method associated with the post-modernist position seeks to sacrifice the idea of a professional, expert voice and to encourage the client's fullest participation and invention of new possible meanings in the conversation that will occur between them. When the therapist does ask questions or make statements they will tend to begin comments with phrases like, 'Could it be that . . .?' or 'What if . . .?' rather than, 'This is a case of . . .' or 'What you need to do . . .'. In its widest form, therefore, social constructionism seeks to maintain a plurality of stories and possibilities of story organization which keep meanings fluid and unfixed. It constantly seeks to resist the tendency for accounts to be perceived as true versions, as privileged discourses which would result in their acquiring a rigidity.

In this new era of post-modernism professional counsellors are therefore no longer in a position of making decisions for or about clients. Rather they may offer opinion on technical information, they may offer their view, but they never have the right (for example through reference to some guiding theory or other esoteric 'discourse') to impose that view nor undermine or de-value the view expressed by the client. *The process of counselling is therefore to facilitate the development of a conversation which allows the client in its centre to make some decision about how they may perform the next period of their lives.*

In order to provide a overview of the relevance of social constructionism to counselling Table 3 is presented.

Table 3: Social Constructionism

Attributes of Social Consructionism	Non-attributes
S.C. provides a conceptual context for understanding the counselling relationship	S.C. is not a new type of therapy or even a set of therapeutic techniques
S.C. deals with theory, personal accounts, and other evidence in terms of its usefulness rather than in terms of truth or external validity	S.C. is not a licence for saying all views are equally legitimate or persuasive
S.C. recognizes that individuals will have preferences for particular ways of viewing experiences etc	S.C. does not accept that these personal choices constitute truth or reality statements
S.C. proposes that personal knowledge derives from participation in social interaction via participation in conversation, social exchange and holds that problems are generated by and embedded in current patterns of meaning and interaction rather than being products of inside (the individual) or outsides forces	S.C. is not a restriction requiring that the counsellor does not hold a view nor that references to social structures, and social 'realities' and individual characteristics cannot be made
S.C. proposes that instructive interaction cannot have a certain outcome, i.e. what the 'expert' tells the 'non-expert' does not determine what the non-expert then comes to believe, know or do	S.C. does not require that the counsellor never assumes an expert role or relationship with the client
S.C. supports the view that counselling is constructive rather than remedial	S.C. is not consistent with a view that counselling repairs faulty people or social systems
S.C. is dependent on the ability and willingness of the counsellor to remain non-attached to rules, structures and personal preferences in order to be free to consider and propose other ways of describing what appears to be happening	S.C. does not require that the counsellor remains personally neutral or passive to the information received
S.C. seeks to understand the concepts, rules and structures of the client's experiences and story	S.C. is not preoccupied with the construction of explanatory or causal schema
Understanding is always interpretative since S.C. insists there is no privileged standpoint for understanding	S.C. is not simply a reframing of people's accounts with 'superior' versions

SYSTEMIC IDEAS AND COUNSELLING

No matter what theoretical and therapeutic framework the counsellor refers to, there is always a recognition, sometimes by the client and always by the counsellor, that individual experience necessarily involves and refers to other people. Whatever view of the individual we subscribe to it must make links somewhere to their histories and relationships. The notion of inter-relatedness is thus implied or explicit in all clinical psychological theory. Inter-relatedness is a defining feature of systems but systemic thinking refers to far more than this since the notion of *interdependency* implies a further step into the nature of social embeddedness as it refers to reciprocal and circular causal processes. Family systems theory provides such a conceptual scheme and is founded upon a number of basic ideas which refer to a system's wholeness, organization and circular interactional processes. The 'task' for the systemic counsellor and systemically informed counselling is to find a way of conceptualizing the *wholeness, organization, change and circular patterns of transaction* which describe the individual client's social and historical context.

Wholeness

Families are open social systems which by cultural convention may be distinguished from other social systems. In fact as we shall see the distinctions are, in systemic terms, arbitrary, though nonetheless useful to the tasks of understanding and describing. Family characteristics (principally those of self-regulation) are not reducible to the characteristics of individual members. Each member to some extent will be constrained by relationships with others but no one person is entirely explained in terms of the 'other'. This idea is well expressed in the phrase, 'A system is more than the sum of its parts (i.e. individual members' characteristics).' By speaking of the wholeness of any system we are stressing the inseparably integrated, complex relatedness of its components. A family's integrity and social continuity is an expression of its wholeness and is encapsulated in the statement, 'I am not entirely defined by my family membership but an event or change within it will always affect me in some way and vice versa.' All members are therefore participants in family processes of change or stability even though the 'trigger' which perturbs the family system may not arise within their own personal experience. An individual's experience, however, will always have repercussions in his/her family.

Organization

Families within and across cultures and within a culture's history vary in the patterns of interaction which illustrate their internal organization. For the family system to maintain integrity some ordering processes must occur. Individual members contribute to the formation of family patterns of interaction and in a reciprocal manner their behaviour is organized by participation in those patterns. The appearance of distinct 'rules' of interaction and understanding within certain family relationships is a particular example of systemic organization. Various relationships within the family therefore may be described as subsystem relationships when the rules allow or create 'boundaries' of status, function and of course membership. In terms of the whole family however, there will also be evident, in its characteristic expressions and interactions, a discernible overarching organization.

Minuchin (1985) writes of families responding to events in ways that define them as differentiated wholes and she also comments on a 'family style' which are its recurrent patterns of interaction. 'Family style' has also been referred to as 'family structure' and indicates the 'rules' of interaction which organize the family's behaviour. These rules of interaction have led to stylistic dimensions being described such as enmeshment, levels of flexibility and cohesiveness etc. Attempts have been made to identify *universal* dimensions of structure or style as well as to fix certain patterns of organization onto particular kinds of dysfunctioning families (Olsen *et al.*, 1988). These are reminiscent of attempts in the psychology of the individual to specify universal personality types and disorders and similarly it has been discovered that the quest is unachievable. This is because it is fundamentally contradictory as no matter at what systemic level one considers (individual/nuclear family/extended family) a continuous process of change occurs, which prevents the defining of any phenomenon as permanently stable.

Change

Open systems are dynamic. They may demonstrate characteristic patterns of interaction but these patterns are not constant across time or contexts. In particular a reorganization of patterns will occur when events challenge the adequacy of existing interactional patterns of response. The challenge to adapt may arise out of developmental movement or simply be unpredictable. Within the life cycle a response to the tendency towards organization is seen to occur and re-occur as adaptive stable patterns emerge only then to erode and later to re-emerge in a different or recast form. If the nature of change is generally perceived as gradual and evolutionary, it should not be assumed that changes in patterns are always or necessarily gradual; startlingly rapid change can be precipitated by the nature of 'challenges' to existing organization. The nature of reorganization cannot be easily predicted in such rapid-change situations since a period of 'chaos' can erupt within a family system where pre-existing rules, meanings etc., are completely altered. The period of extreme instability requires very high energy output and is relatively short-lived before stabilizing and new patterns of organization emerge (see Transitions, p. 131).

Circularity

The process through which patterns of stability are maintained and change occurs is circular rather than linear. A cause leads to an effect which automatically becomes another cause. Interactional systems are continuously 'communicating', providing cycles of unbroken feedback between all parts and levels of the system. Family systems communicate, receive communication and indeed *are* communication – there is thus a continuous, endless looping of information exchange throughout the system which has no beginning or end but a spiralling circular movement through time. Indeed it is solely the change in information that produces a change in function of a system. Once it is accepted that the *cycle of interaction* is the 'unit' of the system this, rather than the individual, then becomes the focus and primary source of change. The point is that individuals cannot be considered to be entirely 'free' to act in new ways since they are, to some degree, defined and maintained by the circular interactional pattern of which they are part. From this perspective, it is the meaning about a pattern of an interaction which changes to allow the individual to show new and different forms of behaviour.

In summary, the family is conceived of as an integrated, dynamic, organic entity (system) and though it is constituted of organized, dynamic subsystems, the route to understanding its transformations is through recognizing the recurring patterns of interaction which occur within and between its every level. Possibly the hardest point of all to accept is the idea that getting 'inside' the head and heart of the individual is not a primary or even secondary interest of the radical systems theorist. The unit of greatest interest, even fundamental to an understanding of family, is the cycle of transactions and the meanings ascribed to those transactions by the 'system'.

INDIVIDUAL EXPERIENCE

Family systems theory could be said to have begun as a reaction to the 'science' of developmental psychology and its attempt to measure and explain individual experience as a socially isolated and decontextualized phenomenon. However, family systems theory has opponents who regard it as discounting or relegating individual experience to merely part of a broader interconnected pattern. The systemic view does not overlook or deny individual experience but it does insist that the self is, like all social phenomena, systemically embedded and socially constructed. The systemic and other interactional viewpoints propose that individual identity evolves socially; that all human behaviour is social communication and is embedded within, and at the same time is part of, a continuous system of interpersonal connections. The primary focus of interest of all interactional perspectives is the pattern of connections between individuals. These patterns are regarded as being complementary or interdependent with respect to some outcome. Individual characteristics therefore are considered as the behaviour illustrating the connection rather than something located within the individual. Hence individuals are described as demonstrating certain behaviour rather than being labelled as a particular type of person. Therefore to say that a person is 'blunt' does not capture the sense of all the interactions around him or her at a particular time, it is more accurate to report that when certain interactions occur the person *displays behaviour that may be termed bluntness.*

Individuals develop a capacity for self-observation, of becoming observer to their own behaviour and thoughts, they are capable of self-reflection and self-representation. This capacity is a feature of developmental growth and social experience, and as such it is a capacity which can move between levels of complexity such that the individual can perceive the self, the other or the whole transactional pattern which includes the self. It is the capacity for self-observation which permits individuals to describe themselves, their feelings, ideas, intentions, behaviours to others and to themselves. Often, in response to 'challenging' interactions, e.g. conflicting needs in a relationship, the individual appears to reduce the challenge by exercising a reflexive withdrawal from ongoing events. This psychological retreat is an attempt by the individual to reduce the conflict and 'noise' arising from the interactional context and to focus attention upon his/her own experiences and to plan future action. The egocentric nature of the individual's withdrawal removes him/her from the consciousness of the moment where the on-going activities of others will have important influences on the interactions occurring. This 'time-out' allows the person to work out what he is going to do but the period results in the loss of awareness of how the system is operating. A consequence of planning in this way to deal with challenges is that *the individual relates action to something that is anticipated rather than to the process of the moment.* The degree to which any individual indulges in an excessively focused view of his/her own particular conception of events in the system will determine the extent to which that person is removed from appreciating his position within the functioning system. Within families and couples this happens continually as individuals focus on 'this is what I need', or 'this is what others do to me', rather than considering the process of interaction for the family as a whole or the couple as an entity. Couples and families therefore have the ability to be aware of the social interactive nature of themselves but this awareness requires individuals to subsume their identities within that of the system and unfortunately this does not occur at times when problems and challenges arise. Bateson (1973) notes that even though humans are embedded in biological, ecological, and social systems, there is a twist in the psychology of the individual person whereby consciousness is almost of necessity blinded to our own systemic nature. Even though we are an element of interacting systems we somehow forget it. This finds an echo in developmental processes where an early period of cognitive development is marked by an egocentric approach – an approach that can reappear when the child experiences a form of threat. This appears to be a similar process that continues to operate throughout life, distracting us from our own systemic qualities.

Because every behaviour is at one and the same time an expression of the person and a communication to others (Watzlawick *et al.*, 1974), there is a strong tendency to experience our communications solely as expressions of the self. We emphasize the 'What I do' to the neglect of 'This is my contribution to what we do'. In order for a couple or family to operate successfully there therefore needs to be a negotiation involving each person's contribution. It is by this process that an agreed 'meaning' of the social context for all evolves. As these meanings are constructed then perceptions, opinions, expressions and actions of the 'self' are also changed. Gergen (1982) has discussed the manner in which self-definition realigns over time as social circumstances change. A person's experience of self is so much a social phenomenon, so much a responsive process, that it cannot be imagined to hold constant as families, couples and individuals change and develop.

INDIVIDUAL EXPERIENCE IN THE COUNSELLING SYSTEM

In whatever way we construe the human experience and condition, in counselling the individual's private and personal accounting of

Table 4:   Individual and Systemic Perspectives

Individual Level	Systems Level
A person is not fully described by membership of a family or other social relationships	A family is more than a collection of individual members and their experiences
A person is the primary agent of and responsible for their own behaviour and development	All family members are part of, and defined by, family developmental processes and patterns
Personal and private experience and thoughts encapsulate the 'true' person	People are defined and known by the cycles of interaction in which they participate and of which they are a part

experience must always be genuinely addressed. This is regardless of what systemic patterns of interaction are thought to control and shape its existence. The dilemma facing the counsellor is well conveyed by placing the individual and systemic perspectives side by side (Table 4).

An overly rigid focus on any one level of understanding or description may restrict or threaten the possibility of meeting with the client's view of the position. The counsellor therefore needs to be able to move across and through levels as the therapeutic moment requires even though he/she will at the same time tend to refer to a favoured theoretical base when thinking about the client's position. Whether the moment requires a focus upon the family system or the individual in relationship, the requirement is for an integration to occur across levels of analysis so that the system always implies individual and vice versa.

The systemic counsellor is attentive and considerate of the individual's private and personal account but remains equally mindful of and attentive to 'the systemic' and 'the developmental' in the individual's relaying of his experience. Thus the counsellor will recognize and validate the individual's private and even secret experiences but will also be considering how the individual's position is a function of systemic rules and patterns. This enables the counsellor to 'hold' the client as a 'self-contained' individual and as part of a complex of interdependent integrated relationships.

As systemic counsellors we conceive of the 'task' of conceptualization as being similar to the task of perceiving an optical illusion which trades on foreground–background shift. Both aspects of the illusion are present and remain available to future inspection no matter which version of the illusion is dominant at any one moment. With such an illusion the observer/viewer may:

- see one version only and not know of the other;
- accept there are other versions but is unable to see them;
- become able to see other versions with external guidance;
- see both versions and be able to switch between versions at will.

In systemic counselling the objective would be to help the client to see the fullest picture possible, i.e. both versions/perspectives. This is not the same as saying there is a single and right version; that would be to deny the different levels of perception and meaning. From this perspective it is believed that the counsellor is in the most helpful position to the client if they can see both (many) versions of the world at will and maintain that position even when the individual talks in private and personal terms. Clients may often be unable to perceive more than their own perspective and the broadening and liberating task of counselling/consultation will be to help them locate their account in more straightforward relationship to alternative levels of meaning that are available to them. Different methods of interviewing may be more or less successful at achieving this goal but the method which lends itself most readily is known as interventive interviewing (Tomm, 1987a, b, 1988) (see Consultative Interviewing, p. 148).

THE DEVELOPMENTAL PERSPECTIVE

Whether we are talking about single individuals or whole families the need to apply a developmental perspective and to recognize developmental processes is paramount. Without an awareness of developmental issues the task of achieving an adequate understanding and description of people and their lives lacks depth. Although much remains unclear and inadequately conceptualized in developmental theory its relevance and usefulness to the pursuit of understanding a client's account of their situation and the counselling process is central.

Classical developmental theory isolated the individual and emphasized notions of unvarying and sequential change. With a focus primarily on the early years, developmental stages were seen as progressive and hierarchical, moving towards a zenith in midlife, and thereafter individuals were considered to be functionally declining. Developmental theory has developed since it first attempted to account for change through life and the present paradigm for outlining development is most clearly expressed in the developmental life span perspective (Carter and McGoldrick, 1989). This attempts to offer a less value-based account of human development and to extend the developmental range, as its title implies, across the whole human life span. This perspective can be summarized in terms of its central premises:

- Development is life-long.
- Development is continuous; the rates of developmental change and important social contexts involved in developmental processes vary across the age range.
- Every age period of the life span is a developmentally active one.
- There is no special state of maturity/excellence in human development.
- The processes of change in human life may take on many forms in terms of onset, duration, termination and direction; it is a pluralistic concept of development.
- The self and other interpersonal human systems are in dynamic interaction internally with themselves and externally with the surrounding social context.
- There is always movement towards a fundamental organization of the self-system and larger interpersonal systems, i.e. movement toward the functional integration of person, family, social groups, work organizations.

An example of a specific developmental theoretical model which embraces the new paradigm is found in Bronfenbrenner's ecological system theory (EST). As its basic premise Bronfenbrenner (1989) suggests that,

> the ecology of human development is the scientific study of the progressive, mutual accommodation throughout the life course between an active, growing human being and the changing properties of the immediate settings in which the developing person lives, as this process is affected by the relations between these settings, and by the larger context in which the settings are embedded.

That is, development is seen as a joint function of person and environment. In EST development is construed as those processes through which the person and the environment interact to produce patterns of constancy and change in the characteristics of the person over the life course. Furthermore, the developmental outcomes of today, in recursive manner, also contribute to the shaping of the developmental outcomes of tomorrow. Cause and effect are integrally intertwined. Although Bronfenbrenner's focus is primarily upon the individual EST does incorporate in a statement of its core principles the central and crucial idea that development is not something that happens inside people. People and the characteristics of people can only exist and exert an influence on development in terms of the interaction between the person and the outside world. Every human quality is inextricably embedded socially and finds both its meaning and fullest expression, in particular environmental settings. As a result of this social embeddedness there is always an interplay between the psychological characteristics of the person and a relevant specific environment. The one cannot be defined without reference to the other. This ultimately challenges the notion that some form of constant boundary exists between the person and the environment. In the dynamic processes of development, person and environment are at one and the same time both a unity and separate units with the relative balance being determined by the activity.

Whilst the new developmental paradigm has challenged some of the hidden assumptions of the classical developmental model its focus of interest has also remained on the individual. This concentration on individual is however perhaps more an indication of the limited ability of scientific methodology to describe, measure and test hypotheses about the functioning of complicated interactive interpersonal systems. Theoretical developments are now moving toward a consideration of the relationship, hence we now have a burgeoning field of relationship studies (e.g. Hinde and Stevenson-Hinde, 1987) and relationship theory (Sroufe and Fleeson, 1986). Since the early studies of child development there has been a necessary and inevitable broadening of outlook to include the parent–child relationship. This relationship is now seen to be more than the environment for child development but actually *a part of the process* of child development. Alongside this there is a newly emerging conception of the family also – not again as the mere context for human development but as an organic, dynamic social entity (Minuchin, 1985).

Individual and Family Development

It is within this social complex that, for the sake of convenience, the counsellor must operate and in a sense isolate the individual client from the social and familial context which is part of his/her development. It is important, however, that this context is not, in the counsellor's mind, simply the context for development as this would represent an arbitrary and unjustifiable dislocation of the individual from ongoing developmental processes. To prevent this from happening models such as the family life-cycle model (Carter and McGoldrick, 1989) attempt a broad descriptive outline of the interdependent and dynamic developmental relationships that exist within the family for each individual. To provide descriptions of family development capable of integrating these developmental processes attention must consequently be paid to four conceptually distinct areas of development.

1. *Individual.* The movement of each individual – child, parent, grand-parent, etc. – through his or her unique life cycle.
2. *Relational.* The continuous interaction of these individual life cycles at every moment of the family's life. In this domain it will also be important to identify specific interactions at specific moments in the family's developmental history.
3. *Familial.* The overall developmental motion of the interacting family organization at any moment so a total pattern is discernible relevant to the family life cycle.
4. *Intergenerational.* The interweaving of intergenerational family life cycles, since the young parent in a family of procreation is at the same time an offspring in a maturing family of origin. It should also be noted that the intergenerational family life cycles which interact are not confined to generations of families still alive, since the history and values of one generation may be carried and expressed long after the demise of any previous generation.

At all times in the course of family development therefore there is an interrelationship between the individual, the systemic, and intergenerational lines of development. It is difficult to find a means of conveying this dynamic quality and various attempts have been made to represent the complex interelatedness of the family across generations and time. Unfortunately the final result can only ever be equivalent to a series of stills from a film as they lack movement, depth of field and any connecting dialogue. The interested reader is referred to the diagrams and charts which appear in works such as that of Street (1994), or Carter and McGoldrick (1989).

Transitions: A Key Developmental Concept

The level of description offered by family developmental models are at present less elaborated than the more individually focused accounts found in child developmental theory. However, as Bronfenbrenner and all developmentalists now acknowledge the ultimate goal of developmental theory is to achieve an explanatory account at the systemic level of human relationships. Notwithstanding the sophistication of any developmental framework, there is a necessity to describe and account for processes of change and stability within any system moving through time. To deal with this all models have a tendency to make use of the concept of *transition*. Although there are variations in the elements emphasized and the significance attributed to transitional phenomena there is a unanimous view that an understanding of transitions is central to the task of appreciating the developmental flow of human life. This is obviously a task that is also central to the counsellor/consultant.

When used in a developmental context transition refers to the process of change or instability that occurs when the individual or system moves from one relatively stable pattern to another relatively stable pattern. The term 'pattern' refers to the organization of behaviours, feelings, or meanings apparent at any given time. As the total developmental process is based upon the dynamic relationship between stability and change, transitions are seen as those periods of instability associated with times in the life cycle perceived as having a pivotal significance to the system's future developmental path. Transitions do not include the continuous minor adjustments in the behaviour of the family and its members. However, for each system's development there will always be unique transitional events and contexts that have a meaning and significance solely to the persons involved. These unique transitions will always be placed within a broad cultural patterning of transitions that present themselves to the majority of individuals and families in any society at any given historical time.

Family life-cycle transitions, by their very definition, therefore involve reciprocal, interdependent changes in persons in close emotional relationships. From the family developmental point of view, individual identity is delineated within close relationships, so the changes in relationships require reorganization of the self. Similarly the interpersonal self will be redefined and reintegrated in the process of adapting to family changes during family life-cycle transitions.

Transitions necessarily involve a degree of additional stress within the system which arises from the system's pre-existing patterns of organization and stability when encountering new 'demands'. As the new demand cannot be avoided, the existing arrangements for dealing with demands become experienced as being inadequate or insufficient. Family systems theories suggest transitional demands require a response which achieves second-order systemic change, that is to say, change which is based upon a reorganization of relationships between parts of the system. This is different from first-order change in which only observable behaviour alters rather than the relationships themselves. Nevertheless the initial ripples of transitional change may actually be a series of first-order changes, which are the system's first attempts at responding to the new demands.

Transitions have been classified as normative or non-normative depending upon their predictability in any life cycle. This classification depends on whether there are available 'rules' established in the culture or family for addressing the demand when it arises. For example, in a family which carries the gene for a genetic disorder such as muscular dystrophy, there may well be a developed familial reaction for dealing with the occurrence of the condition in any new-born male child. At a more cultural level, an example would be the 'rules' available about the movement of a grown child away from the family and whether there would be gender differences in this particular developmental step. The distinction between normative and non-normative transitions is however not adequate, as transitions can also be described along other dimensions, such as (a) their significance and meaning to the people involved, (b) their actual event elements, (c) their timing within the life cycle, (d) the period of time 'allowed' for adjustment, (e) the patterns and processes of adjustment which are considered acceptable and optimal. What would appear to be 'similar' transitions will provoke differing levels of disturbance or unease in the family system when they vary along these dimensions. It is this uniqueness that presents and has to be dealt with clinically.

Given the centrality of transitions it would be incorrect to assume that development is only about change. The early preoccupation with a family's flexibility and adaptability in the face of transitional demands has led to the overlooking of a family's ability to maintain stability. The concentration on change neglected the healthy significance of sometimes maintaining things as they are. An interactional systems approach to human development calls for an integration of the tendency towards change and the tendency toward continuity. Indeed it is now recognized that a more adequate theoretical and therapeutic approach must focus upon both stability and change processes rather than a preoccupation with the breaks, interruptions and sudden shifts of family development. Healthy adaptation to and coping with developmental challenges requires an integration or synthesis of the two types of process so that a sense of continuity, identity, and stability can be maintained while new interactional patterns are evolving. Stability and change cannot be separated – they are both sides of the same single systemic coin. A theory of family and individual functioning therefore needs to address change and stability simultaneously and offer alternative explanations for dysfunction other than the idea that families and individuals are 'stuck' and unable to bring about change required of a transition. A family and/or an individual must be both flexible and stable; with the tendency towards change and discontinuity occurring simultaneously with the processes supportive of continuity and stability.

Life transitions must be negotiated by all human systems whether individual or familial; and the 'success' with which transitional demands are negotiated is related to the perceived level of disturbance to a family's functioning. At one time thinking in family systems theory held that families had fixed structures and characteristics and the descripion was of families with high and low levels of adaptability to transition and change. More recent thinking and research evidence (Doherty *et al.*, 1991; Olsen *et al.*, 1988), have challenged the idea that there are fixed amounts of any internal characteristics such as adaptability. In order to define 'who' an individual is or 'what' identifies a family system, the current thinking is that this can not be done in terms of 'constants' of behaviour through time. In common with others Bronfenbrenner suggests that the continuity and characteristics of a system or individual are not primarily expressed through constancy of behaviour over time and place, but through the consistency in the ways the system characteristically varies its behaviour as a function of different contexts. As with other aspects of individual or family functioning the characteristics of dealing with transition and change are a function of context.

Counsellors and Transitions

As we have seen, the concept of development classically implies a final goal and movement directed toward that goal. This view has been criticized by the social constructionist perspective as value laden, incorporating not only contents borrowed from the dominant culture but also the therapist's own developmental preferences. Much as they do with regard to other cultural issues, counsellors should therefore not assume similar paths and goals among families faced with similar life-cycle transitions. Certain transitions within a single family's life cycle may be experienced as seriously challenging the family's adaptational resources and sense of integrity. Other transitions may be hardly experienced at all as they are achieved with relatively little threat. A life-cycle assessment must therefore consider the individual's or family's own preferences along with the life-cycle templates carried in the counsellor's personal, conceptual and cultural views.

As experiences within and between families varies greatly, by identifying particular variables before and during a transition period the degree of distress a family experiences during transitions can be assessed. Such variables include the disruption of scheduled time/life plans, the number of new decisions involving stress among family members and the degree of pre-transition family conflict. Assessing these features can also assist in identifying possible future options available to that family or individual.

Applying a developmental framework is not without problems as it can become too rigid a template if applied without reference to the family's understanding of the new information generated by the 'problem'.

Regardless of theoretical orientation, most family counsellors set about the therapeutic task by attempting to detect life-cycle instabilities and through focusing on them attempt to facilitate a situation that will set in motion developmental processes that achieve new balances in the troubled dimensions of a family's life. There is in this orientation a tendency to be over-attentive to the presence of patterns associated with sudden change and as we have seen an undervaluing of processes associated with the maintenance of continuity. Falicov (1988) has suggested that counsellors must bear in mind the dynamic balance that appears to hold between continuous and discontinuous changes at all points in the family life-cycle. At different times and in different areas the balance will change toward more continuity and less discontinuity or vice versa, but one process can never wholly extinguish or replace the other. Only the clients themselves will appreciate the exact balance and this has to be borne in mind continually. Also some counsellors will consider that the 'symptom' indicates a family difficulty in making a life-cycle transitional movement. Although this idea is helpful in moving problem behaviours into an interactional frame again it can be problematic if too rigid a construction is applied. The connection between a family's difficulties, their symptoms and their developmental progress needs to be made more available to them. One possibility is that the symptom itself has a meaningful function or indeed acts as a 'solution' that serves to maintain stability in the face of impending change. Another possibility is that the symptom is a function of the family's organization around the problem which prevents it from adapting to new developmental requirements. A third way of connecting the symptom and developmental progress is to regard the symptom as a manifestation of the stress a family is experiencing in the course of transitional movement. These various possible meanings are rooted in different processes of development and may have quite different implications for therapeutic intervention. Eventually, however, it will be the family's own meaning that will direct the thinking around the problem and the counsellor's task will be to assist them in the formation of their view so that the 'path' of the intervention can be determined.

Bearing in mind the above points it is possible to identify core elements of a family developmental counselling perspective.

Firstly there is a need for the counsellor to be aware of the current stage of the family life cycle with which a family presents. This should be in conjunction with an anticipation of approaching stages of family development, as these will represent opportunities to try out new ways of responding to transitional phenomena.

Secondly the counsellor must have an awareness of the family's current balance of continuity and change-promoting processes and how the family views this.

Thirdly the counsellor needs to have an awareness that developmental progress (change or continuity) is based on the family finding a response to 'information' organized by existing patterns of meaning and requiring the emergence of new patterns of meaning.

Consultation and Transitions

Family counselling may be based on any one of a number of models and the aims of counselling may vary between orientations, family presentations, etc. However, the counselling process from the perspective outlined here is seen clearly as an adjunct to the developmental processes of the family and in broad terms may pursue a number of possible objectives:

- It may attempt to reduce the stressful impact of transitions.
- It may aim to limit or prevent the development of negative chain reactions arising out of transitional change.
- It may seek to establish and maintain the individual's or system's sense of competence and esteem.
- It may seek to identify the future developmental options (including stability) available to the individual or family.

In the brief therapeutic consultation model described here it is the latter objective which is primary. Of course the developmental family model only provides a framework for considering the predictability of family life phases but individual history, trans-generational processes, serendipitous events, etc., will produce the specific developmental processes evident when the client enters counselling or a consulting relationship. The family developmental frameworks have as yet not moved beyond a basic level of description and have much distance to go before they offer a satisfactory account. Higher-level accounts are achieved by philosophical/spiritual arguments that offer systems for explaining the purpose/reasons for events which occur. It must be remembered that it is usually these very questions that clients in their distress are seeking to answer when they enter the consulting relationship. The developmental family frameworks are in no position to offer wider explanations. However, they have a utility in perhaps helping the client and counsellor/consultant to recognize the broader pattern of events and in particular their location and part in continuous developmental processes. One of the central objectives of

the therapeutic consultation is to facilitate the client's linking of disturb-
ing and uncomfortable events to some more meaningful system or code
to which they themselves have ready access. To achieve this client expectations of the social context of counselling/consultation have to be fully
explored.

MODELS OF HELPING AND CLIENT EXPECTATIONS

A recurring theme in many accounts of effective client–professional contact relates to the degree of correspondence that occurs between what the
client expects of the contact and what the professional does. In bald terms
the closer professional action 'fits' with client expectation the more satisfied the client is likely to be and the more successful they will evaluate the
contact (Schwartz and Bernard 1981). Occasions will always arise when
the professional cannot for ethical, professional, resource, or even personal reasons, meet the client expectations of themselves. However, a less
overt reason for making counsellor objectives primary over client expectations may derive from the pursuit of counselling 'ingredients' shown to
be associated with a positive outcome. Garfield (1982) and Elliott (1985)
have both suggested similar 'ingredients' and as the list below shows
they have an immediate face validity:

- activities which promote client insight;
- activities which allow for client emotional expression;
- activities which increase client understanding;
- activities which reinforce and support client qualities, ideas, etc.;
- activities which allow the client to confront and modify ideas, behaviours, etc.;
- activities which provide the client with a credible rationale for a problem's occurrence and for its resolution;
- activities which allow the client to develop and extend their self-coping
  repertoire.

The point to be emphasized is not that these elements are unhelpful to
counselling but that they may be of little value or even insulting to a client
whose expectations do not include a full counselling relationship. These
are activities therefore to be held in abeyance until the client has made an
informed commitment to counselling.

The question for counsellors is how they intend to deal with client expectations. It has been proposed by Strong (1968) initially and noted by many

others since (e.g. Nelson-Jones, 1988) that counsellors are in the business of influencing clients to develop certain views, take certain actions etc. It is in the process of influencing that the goals of counselling are identified by the counsellor and invariably the ambition will tend toward the goal of problem-resolution. However, as Strong has pointed out, the amount of influence to which a client is open will depend on much more than the persuasive skills of the counsellor as critically it will also depend upon the degree of congruence that the client perceives to exist between his/her own view of the problem and potential solutions and the view being expressed by the counsellor. For example, a client who perceives a problem and its solution completely in terms of past experience and the need for changes in his/her own internal, personality characteristics may struggle to accept a counsellor whose orientation and persuasive message is to frame the solution in external, interpersonal action. It seems likely that in such an encounter the counselling relationship will remain exceedingly delicate or indeed never develop.

Various studies looking at 'successful' counselling relationships have supported the view that a good outcome is more likely where a client and counsellor perceive a problem and its solution in a similar manner. It is also evident that it is most often the client who has changed, gradually developing a new account of their difficulty which eventually matches with the one proposed by the counsellor. The underlying process therefore appears to be one where the 'expert' counsellor persuades the client to adopt a new or at least modified view of their problem and of potential solutions. The activity of counselling should therefore be not only portrayed as involving persuasive interpersonal processes but also as being underpinned by the counsellor's use of expert status, power and advantage over the client. Stated in these terms the claims for successful or effective counselling outcomes become important because anything other than a positive outcome may lead to questions about or charges of 'brainwashing', oppression through subjugation, etc. Indeed criticism along these lines can easily be developed from the social constructionist position (see The Social Constructionist View of Counsellor–Client Relationship, p. 116).

Brickman *et al.* (1982) have suggested that common mismatches in expectation arising in counselling can be related to what they have termed the four basic 'models of helping' (Table 5). These are the common conceptual and attitudinal models of helping held by clients and professionals. The four primary models he labels as the moral, the medical, the compensatory and the enlightenment models of helping. These can be applied to the counselling relationship in terms of the way they account for the process of change and the location of responsibility for the development of a solution to the client's difficulty.

Table 5:   Models of Helping

Model	Responsibility Role	Reciprocal Role
1. Medical	*Professional* responsible for the solution	*Client* is to passively receive
2. Moral	*Client* responsible for the solution	*Professional* role is to motivate the client to maintain change efforts
3. Compensatory	*Client* and *professional* jointly responsible for the solution	
4. Enlightenment	*Client* responsible for the solution	*Professional* is to make client aware of responsibility and to instil self-discipline

Brickman *et al.*, suggested that a mismatch over perceived responsibilities between client and professional often lies behind reported counselling failures and frustrations. Professionals in a dual role relationship to the client, e.g. teacher and counsellor, are particularly vulnerable to the possibility of a mismatch because in one role they are principally directing the client while in the counsellor role they may wish to assume a more subtle and facilitative role. In general terms it is the compensatory perspective of a joint, collaborative relationship which best encapsulates the principles of a counselling relationship. When the client begins from another perspective an early task for the counsellor might therefore be construed as persuading them to adopt the compensatory outlook. The potential for a fundamental mismatch between client and professional is most certainly present in every counselling relationship and before embarking on a solution designed to produce change the professional must establish the model of helping being applied by the client.

Stages of Change Model

Even when the client and professional share a congruent view with respect to the model of helping – and even when the client has been persuaded to adopt the counsellor's view of the problem and solution possibilities, the risk of mismatch still remains. The stages of change model developed by Prochaska and DiClemente (1982) identifies the major phases of a 'change cycle' which maps the progress of a client in terms of their readiness to change from a phase of not acknowledging they have

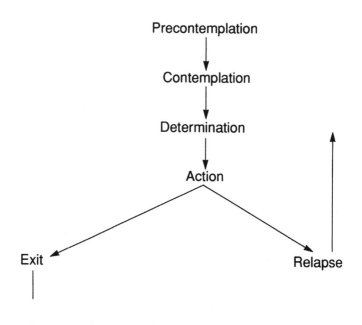

Figure 1:   Readiness to Change Cycle

a problem to a point where the problem has completely resolved. These stages in terms of their relation to each other is set out in Figure 1.

Each stage in the cycle is characterized by different features which require the counsellor to conceive of their overall task as a series of separate functions. The tasks relevant to each phase will therefore of necessity be different and the counsellor will need to demonstrate a different constellation of skills for each phase. The characteristics of each stage are presented in Table 6.

Studies conducted by Prochaska and others, e.g. McConnaughy *et al.* (1989), have provided strong evidence for the presence of the identified stages and attested to the utility of the model. Prochaska and DiClemente claim the stages of change model is transtheoretical and applicable to any process of personal change. The empirical evidence very strongly suggests that even though people may occupy more than one stage of change in respect of a particular issue the majority of their energy will be invested in a principal stage. Similarly it has been found that clients do not necessarily move from one stage to another as they may remain at a particular stage consistently. Generally this does indicate that vacillation between stages as well as ambivalence about movement is evident and

Table 6:   Stages of Change

Stage	Characteristics	Counsellor tasks
Precontemplation: not yet considering the possibility of change	If told has a problem more surprised than defensive or dismissive	Raise doubt Provide information Offer feedback
Contemplation: the person both considers change and rejects it	The existence of ambivalence action strategies engender resistance	To tip the balance in favour of change
Determination: desire for things to be different	A short-lived stage, if no movement into action then there is a return to contemplation	Matching the clients' state – outline change strategies that are acceptable, accessible, appropriate and effective
Action	The counselling or therapy stage or self-initiating action	Availability of suitable strategies and necessary support
Maintenance: sustaining change accomplished by the previous action	Different skills to action stage	Identify and use strategies to prevent relapse
Relapse	These are normal occurrences	Avoid discouragement Renew determination Resume action
Exit		Allow for return under different conditions Clearly terminate current contact

normal. Actual progress across stages appears to be sequential and invariant; a client for example cannot begin taking action over a problem without first passing through a phase of contemplation and then determination.

The importance of the stages of change model for counselling is that it requires the counsellor to carefully consider viable goals for the counselling relationship which depend upon the client's position in terms of his readiness to change. The most common mismatches to occur are when the client is in contemplation stage and the counsellor is offering an action-focused solution or alternatively when the client is in action stage but the counsellor is more concerned with reviewing the causes and meanings of problem elements (e.g. Llewelyn, 1988). In either case the counselling relationship will be under strain and probable rupture unless a shift in focus and emphasis can be achieved. In the early period of contact therefore, the counsellor must attend closely to client communications which indicate the stage of change they predominantly occupy and the need to undertake this clearly has for us resulted in the development of the consultation approach. It will be noted that two of the central aims of the consultation interview are to establish the role the client foresaw for the consultant and to identify jointly with the client his position in the stages of change.

THERAPEUTIC IDEAS RELEVANT TO THERAPEUTIC CONSULTATIONS

Brief Family Therapy

Within the field of systemic family therapy the work by Weakland and the the Palo Alto group (Weakland *et al.*, 1974) is seen as providing a seminal account of an interactional approach to therapy which attempts to prevent the excesses of repeated appointments. The key to this brief therapy is not principally its duration but its focus and methods. In particular brief therapy aims to achieve an outcome, based on the use of existing client patterns (health assumption), which is 'satisfactory' to the client; thus total resolution or second-order levels of change are not automatically pursued. Also it was not expected that 'families' would always be the client as 'the system that maintained the problem' was in a sense the client and hence individuals could very ably be seen. More recently the brief therapy movement has entered a new phase which is represented by the brief solution focused therapy (BSFT) approach. The approach was first described by de Shazer *et al.* (1986) and indicates a shift in emphasis from Weakland's type of brief therapy.

The principles underpinning the BSFT approach are important to outline and are best summarized in a phrase from de Shazer (de Shazer, *et al.*, 1986): 'the aim [of brief therapy] is to start the solution process rather than to stop the complaint pattern.' More specifically key elements are:

- In the client's description of his/her problem are clues to what is being not considered but which if accessed could form the basis of a change (solution) to the original problem.
- By asking questions of the type, 'How would you know the problem had gone? What would be different?' the possibility of change and life without the problem is suggested.
- New and beneficial meanings can always be constructed. These are not presented as the 'real' or 'superior' meanings by the therapist but as

potential plausible alternatives worthy of some consideration. The anticipation is that the client, not the therapist/counsellor, will select whichever meaning appeals most.

- A successful solution does not depend upon an exhausting detailed account of the situation, nor a rigorous account of how the problem is maintained. More important are the changes in interactions around the problem possible within the client's and the context's own constraints, i.e. actions, thoughts, feelings which '*fit*' within the constraints of the total situation.
- Standard systemic ideas about change remain fundamental to the approach. That is, there is an assumption that change in any part of the client's system, no matter how small or apparently insignificant, will effect change in the 'system as a whole' and potentially lead on to profound differences.

Personal Construct Theory

In his theory of personal constructs, Kelly (1955) suggests that for any two people to interact effectively, they need not necessarily share the same constructs but they should have some constructs about how the other sees the world. So not only do we have a theory about the world from our perspective but in order to relate to another person we have a theory about the perspective of the other. Couples and families differ in the rules they have about the inter-relationship of theories. For example, some families have a belief that only one view is correct and different perspectives are not possible; in other families there is a looser ideology on how different individual members are permitted to express difference.

The similarity of two individuals' constructs and the view each individual has of the other's constructions obviously interrelate in a manner that produces interactions of a varying nature. These interactions are particularly important when one considers this framework in its application to the relationship between the consultant and client. We will consider this relationship as the example for considering ideologies in interaction.

1. Should two individuals have different constructs and be inaccurate in viewing how the other construes the situation, they will be in conflict. This conflict may or may not be overtly expressed but the possibility of beginning a negotiation about collaborative joint action will be problematic. This situation will arise for the consultant when he has not been able, for whatever reason, to work with the client's words and constructs and uses in its stead his own view of the situation. Clearly

there will be problems in the consultant being helpful for the client in this situation.

2. If two individuals have similar 'shared' constructs but are inaccurate in viewing how the other construes the situation, then a conflictual situation is again present. In order for the individuals to establish any joint action they would need to appreciate the nature of their shared constructs. In the consultant/client area this situation will occur where the consultant feels uncertain about the accuracy of his understanding of the clients ideology or where the consultant has not communicated his understanding well so that the client does not experience the shared nature of the constructs. Both these situations point to the need for on-going supervision and training for consultants who embark on this work.

3. If the individuals have different constructs and are reasonably accurate in viewing their differences then the basis for beginning to negotiate joint action will be present. In terms of our field of work this is not consultation, though it may be a component of the final stages of the consultative process. Essentially this type of interaction could be seen as being typical of that between a professional and a client where the professional may be able to offer specific services or may be able to suggest to the client where they might be able to obtain certain services.

4. When two individuals have similar shared constructs and are reasonably accurate in viewing how the other sees a particular situation then the individuals will tend to act in unison about the situation. This is the context the consultant wishes to establish within the consultation process. The consultant identifies and elaborates the clients' view of the world, including their view of the consultation process itself, and by communicating this accurately is able to help the client identify strategies to deal with the difficulty that are accessible and acceptable.

Structured Brief Therapy – The Two Plus One Model

Within the individual counselling field the development of briefer forms of therapy/counselling has recently been expressed in the two-plus-one model of therapy described by Barkham (1989). The foundation for this model of counselling practice is very much within those findings which indicate clients may have a quite different ambition for the counselling relationship than the one traditionally identified by the professional viewpoint. Its origin derives from the principal elements of brief therapy as identified by two of its earliest practitioners (Bloom, 1992;

Mann, 1984) both working from a psychodynamic perspective. These elements state:

- Brief therapy attends to one focal issue.
- The focal issue is presented by the client as the reason for coming for help.
- The therapist does not underestimate the client's capacity for change.
- The therapist does not over-estimate a client's level of self-awareness.
- The therapist should be prudently active – asking questions which clarify, listen, summarize, avoid lectures and *self-disclosure*.
- The initial contact should start a problem-solving process.
- The therapist should not take up or interpret transference phenomena, only those aspects of positive transference needed to maintain a supportive and encouraging atmosphere.
- The duration of brief therapy is defined by the client's sense that enough has been accomplished.

Based on these general elements the two-plus-one model presents itself as a model of change and draws upon various schools of thought, but at its heart are two basic approaches to clients' difficulties: the conversational model (Hobson, 1985) and a problem-solving approach (e.g. Spivack *et al.*, 1976). From the former the two-plus-one model takes the idea that the client is in charge of the therapeutic process, a process construed primarily as being a meeting between people who wish to share ideas and experiences in a non-prejudiced and undogmatic manner in the belief and hope that the exchange will be interpersonally enhancing. From the problem-solving approach the two-plus-one model takes forward the idea that most clients enter therapy desirous of solutions to their problems rather than intent on seeking fundamental personal change (Elliott, 1985; Llewelyn, 1988). In broad terms the problem-solving approaches take as focus the client-presented problem and offer the client a process template for tackling difficulties which they then teach the client to use in relation to their problem(s).

The added element to this model is that it draws on research and clinical evidence (Wolberg, 1980) which indicates a planned break in the sequence of contacts between client and therapist is itself helpful to the client's process of change. The implication is that the impact of the counselling sessions may take time to germinate but in a pre-planned period of separation, the client can engage in an independent appraisal of the experiences, ideas, advice etc., and take it forward in his/her own way. Clearly this links with the standard practice of most family therapies which leave large gaps (relative to individual therapies), between sessions in the belief that more 'work' is done between sessions than in them. The crucial features being exploited in the two-plus-one model are its organization – two closely sequenced sessions and a third at some months distance from the second contact – with the presentation of the 'break' being an integral part of the counselling process.

Whilst the coming of briefer therapies may be a welcome indication that the counselling professions are accepting that the client's point of view is a legitimate and authentic frame for the counselling relationship, there remains within them a preoccupation with the promotion of change and, of course, with the delivery of a relationship-based service called therapy or counselling. We contend that the provision of therapy and a concern for 'real' change is still a part of the professional's uninspected agenda, and this may not fit with the agenda brought by the client.

Attempts at Integration: System Levels and Individuals

The rise of briefer therapies does appear to herald a growing respect and practical acknowledgement of the client's expectations and needs of counselling. The issue raised by brief therapies, however, is what happens when a client does expect something more extended, more fundamental and personally focused? Have the brief therapies effectively denied the client access to more traditional forms of therapy? At the same time as brief therapies were being developed there was, it seems, a general drift among counsellors and psychotherapists toward more eclectic methods of working. This may have been provoked by the failure of the existing therapeutic frameworks to satisfactorily explain client difficulties or to provide 'success' in counselling with clients. As we noted earlier the choices appeared to be longer and longer counselling, briefer counselling or more pragmatic client shaped counselling. Dryden (1984) cautions against assuming that 'eclecticism' describes common activities, all of which are necessarily beneficial. For example in 'haphazard eclecticism' the practitioner appears to forsake or downgrade the importance of theory and the counselling relationship in favour of technique-based practice. Pinsof (1994) argues that there is an unpredictability, unaccountability and potential incoherence to a totally eclectic and atheoretical model and this is ethically and professionally insupportable. Increasingly, however, there appears to be a move within the eclectic ranks to develop an integrated model of counselling practice. This attempts to incorporate an array of therapeutic styles and methods bound together with a theoretical view of the counselling relationship and process. Pinsof (1994) has attempted to develop just such a model of eclectic therapy, integrative problem-centred therapy (IPCT). This framework offers the client the genuine possibility of brief, medium- or long-term counselling.

Pinsof's IPCT approach derives from an epistemological base very similar to our own in that it is founded upon theoretical ideas central to social constructionism and systemic theory, namely:

1. an objective reality is ultimately unknowable and absolute or 'true' statements of experience are impossible. There are therefore multiple versions of experience/reality.
2. people are part of organized larger systems which are maintained through processes of mutual causality (circular, reciprocal, inter-actional).

The therapeutic approach is then set upon four basic premises, which in social constructionist terms are not 'facts' but assertions of belief guiding actions and shaping new beliefs.

- In IPCT the focus is always on the 'problem' as presented by the client.
- The client is healthy and has access to health-giving resources; he/she can therefore solve the problem with the least help necessary from the therapist.
- Therapy should always start with the simplest therapeutic intervention possible. More complex and fundamental attempts at change should only emerge if earlier interventions 'fail'.
- The 'problem' takes its existence from a problem-maintenance context which includes all those factors apparently linked with it. However, until proven otherwise the problem-maintenance context is assumed to be superficial and simple.

For IPCT the first task is always to develop an agreed view of the problem and to proceed to the offering of simple behavioural advice focused on change producing effects. Increasing therapeutic 'depth' is required only by the revelation that simple formulations and methods are inadequate. For IPCT the movement in therapeutic method is always from behavioural to experiential to historical focus and the context for problem-maintenance from family system to same-generation dyads (marital) and finally to individual.

This model coincides in a number of places with the method of working outlined in this book. However, the IPCT still upholds a view that if little does not 'work' then more is needed and in this presumption appears to neglect the possibility that the client may disagree with the evaluation of initial efforts or the need to proceed further – now or ever – in therapy.

Theoretically integrated models of eclectic practice such as the IPCT (or Beutler's (1983) eclectic model) are bound together by the principle that therapy/counselling must follow client need as closely as possible. However, and as with all the models of therapy/counselling described to this point, the importance of meeting clients in a pre-therapy, consultative space is overlooked. It is within this space that some possibility of meeting the client as 'equal but different' is more likely.

Consultative Interviewing

Tomm (1987a, b, 1988) and other authors, (e.g. Andersen, 1987; Goolishian, 1992), have given much thought to how the professional can conduct a therapeutic interview in such a way that the client develops the potential for viewing his/her own position, from another (or many other) angle(s). Since they all base their understanding and approach within a systems framework an initial and uniting idea is that the counsellor, on meeting with the client, is immediately intervening in the client system and actually becomes part of the system's interactions. From this point of view the question is not whether to intervene but how to intervene and to what degree. Tomm (1987a), takes this view the furthest in discussing 'interventive interviewing', a perspective in which 'everything an interviewer does and says, and does not do and say, is thought of as an intervention that could be therapeutic, non-therapeutic or countertherapeutic.' The final phrase is vital to the view being expressed since it acknowledges that the effect of any intervention will not be determined by the counsellor but by the client and the systemic context. In Maturana's terms (Maturana and Varela, 1980) the receiver's/client's response is 'structurally determined', i.e. limited by how they know and how they understand. Tomm (1987a) therefore has developed the original ideas of 'circularity, hypothesizing, and neutrality', (Selvini-Palazzoli et al., 1980) and raised the interventive significance of therapist action and requiring therapists to reflect on all their actions, not just those which might previously have been described as intentional interventions (Tomm, 1987a,b, 1988). Tomm thus proposes that the therapist must learn to use a variety of attitudinal and perceptual postures which by their nature 'support a particular pattern of thoughts and actions and implicitly inhibits others'. For example the hypothesizing posture focuses intellectual efforts on the creation of explanatory accounts, other postures being of circularity, neutrality and strategizing. It is the posture of neutrality which is most central to an effective therapeutic consultation interview.

The position of neutrality is *intended* by the therapist but *ascribed* by the client, i.e. unless the client or family experience the therapist as neutral, therapists cannot claim to have been successful in their intent. Further-more in any social interaction it is impossible to maintain absolute neu-trality since any action or non-action is a communication at some level which may be seen as affirming or disagreeing with another's statement, action, etc. The idea and intention of a neutral posture is to become immersed in experiencing the present interaction as fully and openly as possible, accepting everything that occurs as necessary and inevitable, including the client's and the therapist's own constructions. Neutrality is thus founded on an acceptance of 'what is' and 'is not' rather than being concerned with what 'ought to be'. From within this posture it is possible to be affirming of individuals and their accounts, without becoming com-mitted to or repulsed by what they do or describe. In this respect there is a similarity with traditional, non-directive Rogerian counselling since this correlates with a position of unconditional positive regard, empathy and acceptance (see Street, 1994). Perhaps the whole point and very essence of the neutral consultant/therapist is to avoid what Bateson (1973) called the 'inherent blindness and lack of wisdom in too much purpose'. Being purposeful fosters the development of ideas about the correctness and certainty of particular perspectives and limits the capacity to experience 'other views and possibilities'. The posture of neutrality is not sufficient in itself to stimulate the possibility of the client developing broader or alternative views of their position. This possibility is pursued through the posing of reflexive questions which are composed, timed and asked by the therapist with the intent of activating the reflexivity which exists between the meanings and values present in the client's existing belief system. By stimulating a possible change in meaning at some point or level in the belief system the individual or family is laid open to the possibility of generating new patterns of meaning and behaviour of their own. The meanings or patterns are 'encouraged' by the reflexive ques-tions asked and cannot be prescriptively laid down by the therapist. Once new meanings come into existence new interactions develop.

THE WRITTEN WORD IN THERAPEUTIC ENCOUNTERS

There is a distinctive role for written correspondence in the essentially oral tradition of professional counselling. Written communication has properties of form and meaning which make it distinct from the spoken word and to some extent autonomous from it (Stubbs, 1980). In particular written language tends to use a more precise grammar, more complete sentences, more clearly developed themes and a wider vocabulary than the spoken word. Overall written communications, in the form of letters, will evidence a clearer construction of central purpose, whether that be the expression of ideas, argument or the recording of events. In addition, in all cultures where writing has become the principal medium for transmitting information and knowledge, the written communication has, in general terms, been given a status of higher authority and significance when compared with the spoken word. The heightened status of the written word has been possibly underpinned by the legal importance attached to formal signed documents. In essence, the written word is taken as incontrovertible proof that something has been stated by its author to the recipient. It is, even when a private communication, ultimately tangible, portable and publicly examinable. The author passes thoughts and words, in concrete and static form – though their meaning always remains open to diverse interpretation – into the hands and *ownership* of the recipient. In so doing the correspondence may achieve a number of things less easily achieved by conversational exchange.

Perhaps a distinguishing feature of consultations and an essential element of therapeutic consultations is the consultant's written summary of meetings and conversations with the consultee in which the consultant offers an account of the matters brought to them by the consultee. The use of letters in 'therapeutic consultations' is however more than simply an observation of established convention taken from the traditional commercial model of consultation found in the business setting. The primary function of written communication in therapeutic consultations is to confirm the consultees' independence from the consultant and the consultative dialogue and to underscore their autonomy when making their next decision. A letter of this sort is therefore more of an extension of the *conversational* exchange rather than simply a summary of past conversations between the consultant and consultee. A letter about a conversation shifts the balance of the relationship into a formal arena of exchange. Verbally conducted meetings can, of course, be formal or intimate but an extended conversation, particularly in the counselling setting, will always move towards an increasingly secure intimacy, based upon trust between the participants. This movement towards intimacy also occurs in a therapeutic consultation but there is a need in consultation to reassert the client's independence and decision-making power. The effective letter will convey the sense of intimacy achieved by the participants through the use of personal pronouns, personal phrases of the client and its empathic tone but, in being written and then delivered to the client's home, it automatically signifies that a more formal communication is occurring.

The client, once in receipt of a letter, is then the *owner* of the letter and its contents. The clients can do things with it, in private or public, which underlines their freedom from the letter's author. They may read and re-

read it, they may read and re-read certain passages, they may write on it themselves or they make 'look up' words. In addition they may choose to show the letter to others, to invite their thoughts and responses to the ideas expressed in the letter. In the very act of reading, as opposed to verbally conversing, an independence between written word, message and reader is achieved. This confirms a key aspect of consultation which is the client's equal status and freedom to choose the next steps.

At a simple but vitally important level a letter, compared to a spoken exchange, will invariably improve the client's memory for content and understanding of message. Clients demonstrate poor recall of information received in medical settings, particularly of messages with a high information content, but in studies comparing spoken and written communication the superiority of the written word is well documented (Ley and Morris, 1984). While it may be argued that an opinion offered out of a therapeutic consultation is likely to be less technical and more familiar in content to the client, it would be unjustified to assume that forgetting or 'distortion' of the message will be insignificant.

The field of discourse analysis has demonstrated that interpersonal exchange invariably leads to idiosyncratic accounts varying in emphasis and memory for detail of the interaction (Potter and Wetherall, 1987). This highlights the notion that people in interaction with others will experience a shared event differently and will recall it and possibly attribute it differently. The realm of discourse analysis has also shown that a range of factors – characteristics of participants, the context, the message, the intentions and interests of the participants etc., will consistently but unpredictably bias or distract participants from perceiving some aspects of the interaction and communication and to focus on isolated elements of the total exchange. In consultation the letter will organize the client's story along a temporal and developmental dimension, making clear possible links between the past, present and future aspects of the client's life account. Presenting an account in static form facilitates the client's perception of a gestalt – the facility of written communication to organize and sequence elements and themes further increases the possibility of a total pattern being perceived and new meaning generated. This aspect of written communication between counsellor and client has been developed to its full therapeutic effect by Epston and White (1989).

A related aspect is that a letter is more likely to create an intrapersonal dialogue; a self-reflexive process which may lead the reader into developing a new relationship with his/her own story through being placed in a different relationship to it. An account of one's life in written form necessarily achieves some externalization of personal issues promoting the

Table 7:   Written Correspondence to Clients

- Public and examinable
- In the possession and ownership of the client
- A confirmation of the client's autonomy and independence
- Places the client as reader of the letter in an observer or self-reflexive position to his/her own story.
- Letter assists the client to see a fuller version of his/her own story and to perceive new meanings or patterns in it.

possibility of new meanings and future courses being identified and explored (Maturana and Varela, 1980). This builds upon the letter as a communication which relates to the client's life and situation as he/she reports it but which has been heard and then conveyed in written form by another person from an inevitable slightly different perspective. The 'successful' letter provides the consultees with an account they instantly recognize as their own but which also introduces areas or details previously overlooked or understated. It constructs an account of the client's life which in the 'retelling' of the story potentially expands or modifies previous versions. In the technical language of social constructionism, the consultant's letter seeks to achieve and offer the client an account of his/her life which has rhetorical power and theoretical generativity. That is to say it is a communication which is persuasive and believable in its organization and opens up possibilities previously unseen or unattended to by the client. Futhermore and finally it seems justifiable to send clients letters simply on the grounds that in other professional relationships we routinely communicate in letter to clients, referrers, etc. Why not here?

REFERENCES

Andersen, T. (1987) The reflecting team: dialogue and meta-dialogue in clinical work. *Family Process* **26**: 415–428.

Atkinson, D.R., Worthington, R.L., Dana, D.M. and Good, G.E. (1991) Etiology beliefs, preference for counseling orientations, and counseling effectiveness. *Journal of Counseling Psychology*, **38**: 258–264.

Balint, M., Orstein, P. and Balint, E. (1972) *Focal Psychotherapy*. London, Tavistock.

Barkham, M. (1989) Exploratory therapy in 2+1 sessions: I Rationale for a brief psychotherapy model. *British Journal of Psychotherapy*, **6**: 81–88.

Bateson, G. (1973) *Steps to an Ecology of Mind*. St Alban's, Paladin.

Beutler, L.E. (1983) *Eclectic Psychotherapy. A Systemic Approach*. New York, Pergamon.

Bloom, B.L. (1992) *Planned Short-term Psychotherapy*. Boston, Allyn and Bacon.

Brannen, J., and Collard, J. (1982) *Marriages in Trouble*. London, Routledge.

Brewin, C.R. and Bradley, C. (1989) Patient preferences and randomised clinical trials. *British Medical Journal*, **299**: 313–315.

Brickman, P., Rabinowitz, V., Karuza, J., Coates, D., Cohn, E. and Kidder, L. (1982) *Models of Helping and Coping American Psychologist*, 37.4.368–384.

Bronfenbrenner, U. (1989) *Ecological Systems Theory Annals of Child Development*, **6**: 187–249.

Budman S.H. (ed.) (1981) *Forms of Brief Therapy*. New York: Guilford Press.

Byng-Hall, J. (1985) The family script; a useful bidge between theory and practice. *Journal of Family Therapy*, **7**: 301–305.

Carpenter, J. and Treacher, A. (1989) *Problems and Solutions in Marital and Family Therapy*. Oxford: Blackwells.

Carter, B. and McGoldrick, M. (1989) Overview: the changing family life cycle. In B. Carter and M. McGoldrick (eds). *The Changing Family Life Cycle. A Framework for Family Therapy*, 2nd edition. Boston: Allyn & Bacon.

Cecchin, G. (1987) Hypothesizing, circularity and neutrality revisited: An invitation to curiosity. *Family Process* **26**: 405–413.

Dallos, R. (1991) *Family Belief Systems, Therapy and Change*. Milton Keynes, Open University Press.

Dare, C. and Lindsey, C. (1979) Children in family therapy. *Journal of Family Therapy*, **1**: 253–269.

de Shazer, S., Berg, I., Lipchick, E., Nunnally, E., Molnar, A., Gingerich, W. and Weiner-Davis, M. (1986) Brief therapy: a focused solution development. *Family Process*, **25**: 207–222.

Doherty, W. J., Colangelo, N. and Hovander, D. (1991) Priority setting in family change and clinical practice: the FIRO model. *Family Process*, **30**: 227–240.

Dowling, E. (1993) Are family therapists listening to the young? A psychological perspective. *Journal of Family Therapy*, **15**: 403–412.

Dryden, W. (1984) Issues in the eclectic practice of individual therapy. In W. Dryden (ed.) *Individual Therapy in Britain*, Open University Press: Milton Keynes.

Egan, G. (1990) *The Skilled Helper: A Systemic Approach to Effective Helping*, 4th Edition. Pacific Grove, California: Brooks/Cole.

Elliott, R. (1985) Helpful and nonhelpful events in brief counselling interviews: an empirical taxonomy. *Journal of Counseling Psychology*, **32**: 307–322.

Epston, D. and White, M. (1989) *Literate Means to Therapeutic Ends*. Adelaide: Dulwich Centre Publications.

Falicov, C. J. (1988) Learning to think culturally in family therapy training. In H. Liddle *et al.* (eds), *Family Therapy Training: Recent Trends, Perspectives and Developments*. New York: Guildford Press.

Foucault, M. (1975) *The Archeology of Knowledge*, London: Tavistock.

Foulks, E.F., Persons, J.B. and Merkel, R.L. (1986) The effects of patients' beliefs about their illness on compliance in psychotherapy. *American Journal of Psychiatry*, **143**: 340–344.

Gallessich, J. (1985) Toward a metatheory of consultation. In D. Brown and D. Kurpius (eds) Consultation (Special Issue) *The Counselling Psychologist* **13**: 336–354.

Garfield, S.L. (1982) Eclecticism and integrationism in psychotherapy. *Behaviour Therapy*, **13**: 610–623.

Gergen, K. (1982) *Towards Transformation in Social Knowledge*. New York: Springer-Verlag.

Gergen, K. (1991) *The Saturated Self*. New York: Basics Books.

Gleick, J. (1987) *Chaos*. New York: Penguin Books.

Goolishian, H. (1992) The client is the expert. In S. McNamee and K.J. Gergen (eds) *Therapy as Social Construction*. London: Sage.

Goolishian H. and Anderson, H. (1992) Strategy and intervention versus non-intervention; a matter of theory? *Journal of Marital and Family Therapy*, **18**: 5–15.

Gurman, A.S., Kniskern, D. and Pinsof, W. (1985) Research on the process and outcome of marital and family therapy. In S. Garfield and A. Bergin (eds) *Handbook of Psychotherapy and Behaviour Change*, 3rd Edition. New York: Wiley.

Harre, R. (1984) *Personal Being*. Cambridge, MA.: Harvard University Press.

Hinde, R.A. and Stevenson-Hinde, J. (1987) Interpersonal relationships and child development. Developmental Review, **7**: 1–21.

Hobson, R.F. (1985) *Forms of Feeling: the Heart of Psychotherapy*. London: Tavistock.

Hoffman, L. (1989) The family life cycle and discontinuous change. In B. Carter and M. McGoldrick (eds). *The Changing Family Life Cycle: A Framework for Family Therapy*, 2nd edition. Boston: Allyn & Bacon.

Hoffman, L. (1990) Constructing realities: an art of lenses, *Family Process* **29**(1), 1–12.

Hoffman, L. (1992) A reflexive stance for family therapy. In S. McNamee and K.J. Gergen (eds). *Therapy as Social Construction*. London: Sage.

Howard K.I., Kopta, S.M., Krause, M.S. and Orlinsky, D.E. (1986) The dose effect relationship in psychotherapy, *American Psychologist*, **41**: 159–164.

Kearney, P., Byrne, N. and McCarthy, I. (1989) Just metaphors: marginal illuminations in a colonial retreat, *Family Therapy Case Studies*, **4**: 17–31.

Kelly, G.A. (1955) *The Psychology of Personal Constructs*. New York: Norton.

Ley, P. and Morris, L.A. (1984) Psychological aspects of written information for patients. In S. Rachman (ed.) *Contributions to Medical Psychology*, Vol. 3. Oxford: Pergamon Press.

Littlepage, G.E., Kosloski, K.D., Schnelle, J.F., McNees, M.P. and Gendrich, J.C. (1976) The problem of early outpatient terminations from community health centers: a problem for whom? *Journal of Community Psychology*, 4: 164–167.

Llewelyn, S.P. (1988) Psychological therapy as viewed by clients and therapists. *British Journal of Clinical Psychology*, 27: 223–237.

McConnaughy, E.A., DiClemente, C.C., Prochaska, J.O. and Velicer, W.F. (1989) Stages of change in psychotherapy: a follow-up report. *Psychotherapy*, 26: 4, 494–503.

Mann, J. (1984) Time-limited psychotherapy. In L. Grinspoon (ed.) *Psychiatry update: The American Psychiatric Association Annual Review*, III (pp. 35–44). Washington, DC: American Psychiatric Press.

Maturana, H. and Varela, F.J. (1980) *Autopoeisis and Cognition. The Realization of the Living*. London, Reidel.

Means D. and Thorne, B. (1988) *Person-Centred Counselling in Action*. London: Sage.

Miller, W.R. (1985) Motivation for treatment: a review with special emphasis on alcoholism. *Psychological Bulletin*, 98, 84–107.

Miller, W.R. (1989a) Increasing motivation for change. In R.K. Hester and W.R. Miller (eds), *Handbook of Alcoholism Treatment Approaches: Effective Alternatives*. Elmsford, NY: Pergamon Press.

Miller, W.R. (1989b) Matching individuals with interventions. In R.K. Hester and W.R. Miller (eds), *Handbook of Alcoholism Treatment Approaches: Effective Alternatives*. Elmsford, NY: Pergamon Press.

Miller, W.R. and Jackson, K.A. (1985) Practical psychology for pastors: toward more effective counseling. Englewood Cliffs, NJ: Prentice-Hall.

Minuchin, P. (1985) Families and individual development: provocations from the field of family therapy. *Child Development*, 56: 289–302.

Nelson-Jones, R. (1988) Choice therapy. *Counselling Psychology Quarterly*, 1(1): 43–55.

O'Brien, A. and Loudon, P. (1985) Redressing the balance – involving children in family therapy. *Journal of Family Therapy*, 7: 81–98.

Olsen, D.H., Russell, C.S. and Sprenkle, D.H. (eds) (1988) *Circumplex Model: Systemic Assessment and Treatment of Families*. New York: Haworth Press.

Patterson, G.R. and Frogatch, M.S. (1985) Therapist behaviour as a determinant for client noncompliance: a paradox for the behaviour modifier. *Journal of Consulting and Clinical Psychology*, 53: 6, 846–851.

Perls, F.S., Hefferkubem, R.P. and Goodman, P. (1973) *Gestalt Therapy*. Harmondsworth: Penguin Books.

Pinsof, W.M. (1994) An overview of integrative problem centered therapy: a synthesis of family and individual psychotherapies. *Journal of Family Therapy*, 16: 103–120.

Pistrang, N. and Barker, C. (1992) Client's beliefs about psychological problems. *Counselling Psychology Quarterly*, 5.4.325–335.

Potter, J. and Wetherall, M. (1987) *Discourse and Social Psychology*. London: Sage.

Prochaska, J.U. and DiClemente, C.C. (1982) Transtheoretical therapy. Toward a more integrative model of change. *Psychotherapy Theory. Research and Practice*. 19: 276–288.

Rogers, C.R. (1967). *On Becoming a Person*. London: Constable.

Schwartz, A.J. and Bernard, H.S. (1981) Comparison of patient and therapist evaluation of time-limited psychotherapy. *Psychotherapy*, 18: 101–108.

Selvini-Palazzoli, M., Boscolo, L., Cecchin, G. and Prata, G. (1980) Hypothesizing–circularity–neutrality: Three guidelines for the conductor of the session. *Family Process*, 19: 3–12.

Silverman, W.H. and Beech, R.P. (1979) Are dropouts dropouts? *Journal of Community Psychology*, **7**, 236–242.

Spivack, G., Platt, J.J. and Shure, M. (1976) *The Problem Solving Approach to Adjustment*. San Francisco: Jossey-Bass.

Sroufe, L.A. and Fleeson, J. (1986) Attachment and the construction of relationships. In W. Hartup and Z. Rubin (eds), *Relationships and Development*. Hillsdale, NJ: Erlbaum.

Stiles, W.B., Shapiro, D.A. and Elliott, R. (1986) Are all psychotherapies equivalent? *American Psychologist*, **41** 165–180.

Stiles, W.B., Shapiro, D.A. and Firth-Cozens, J.A. (1990) Correlations of session evaluations with treatment outcome. *British Journal of Clinical Psychology*, **29**: 13–21.

Street, E. (1994) *Counselling for Family Problem*. London: Sage.

Street, E., Downey, J. and Brazier, A. (1991) The development of therapeutic consultations in child-focused family work. *Journal of Family Therapy*, **13**: 311–334.

Strong, S.R. (1968) Counselling: an interpersonal influence process. *Journal of Counselling Psychology*, **15**: 215–224.

Stubbs, M. (1980) *Language and Literacy. The Sociolinguistics of Reading and Writing*. London: Routledge and Kegan Paul.

Tomm, K. (1987a) Interventive interviewing: Part I. Strategizing as a fourth guideline for the therapist. *Family Process*, **26**: 3–13.

Tomm, K. (1987b) Interventive Interviewing: Part II. Reflexive questioning as a means to enable self-healing. *Family Process*, **26**: 167–183.

Tomm, K. (1988) Interventive interviewing: Part III. Intending to ask lineal, circular, strategic or reflexive questions. *Family Process*, **27**: 1–15.

Ursano, R. and Hales, R. (1986) A review of brief psychotherapies. *American Journal of Psychiatry*, **143**: 1507–1517

Waltzlawick, P., Weakland, J. and Fisch, R. (1974) *Change: Principles of Problem Formation and Problem Resolution*. New York: Norton.

Weakland, J., Fisch, R., Watzlawick, P. and Bodin, A. (1974) Brief therapy: focused problem resolution. *Family Process*, **13**: 141–168.

Winnicott, D.W. (1971) *Therapeutic Consultations in Child Psychiatry*. London: Hogarth Press and Institute of Psychoanalysis.

Wolberg, L. (1980), *Handbook of Short-Term Psychotherapy*. New York: Stratton.

Wynne, L.C., McDaniel, S.H. and Weber, T.T. (1987) Professional politics and the concepts of family therapy, family consultation and systems consultation. *Family Process*, **26**: 153–166.

AUTHOR INDEX

SUBJECT INDEX